Kostbare Manschettenknöpfe
Von Pablo Picasso bis James Bond

Precious Cufflinks
From Pablo Picasso to James Bond

Walter Grasser
Franz Hemmerle
Alexander Herzog von Württemberg

Kostbare Manschettenknöpfe
Von Pablo Picasso bis James Bond

Precious Cufflinks
From Pablo Picasso to James Bond

HIRMER

Inhalt
Contents

Walter Grasser, Franz Hemmerle
Kostbare Manschettenknöpfe 12
Precious Cufflinks 13

Walter Grasser
Manschettenknöpfe sind Lebensstil 16
Cufflinks are a Lifestyle 17

Alexander Herzog von Württemberg
Manschettenknöpfe – Schmuck für den Herrn 26
Cufflinks: A Gentleman's Jewelry 27

Kostbare Manschettenknöpfe vom
Ende des 19. Jahrhunderts bis heute 44
Precious Cufflinks from the End of
the 19th Century until the Present Day

    1880–1919   45
    1920–1939   57
    1940–1959   71
    1960–1979   79
    1980–2015   93

Ausgewählte Literatur 115
Selected Bibliography

Bildnachweis 117
Image Credits

Kostbare Manschettenknöpfe

Manschettenknöpfe gehören wie Ringe oder Uhren zu den wenigen Schmuckstücken, die ein Mann stets unangefochten tragen konnte und kann. Im Gegensatz zu Krawattennadeln – die heute aus der Mode gekommen sind – sind diese praktischen wie dekorativen Accessoires nach wie vor beliebt und aus der Welt der Mode nicht wegzudenken. Längst finden sie sich auch nicht mehr nur im Besitz von korrekt gekleideten Herren, sondern zunehmend auch bei modebewussten Damen.

An den Manschettenknöpfen lässt sich der persönliche Schmuckgeschmack ablesen. Sie weisen aber auch auf besondere Vorlieben und Interessen hin: Hierzu zählen Manschettenknöpfe für Autofans, Tennisspieler, Golfer, Jäger, Fischer, Segler und Pferdeliebhaber, aber auch für Handwerksberufe, für Club- und Vereinsmitglieder sowie für Studentenverbindungen, Rotarier, Lions, Freimaurer oder Schlaraffen.

Die ersten Exemplare tauchten bereits im 17. Jahrhundert auf. Gebräuchlich wurden sie aber erst ab dem Ende des 18. Jahrhunderts mit der Weiterentwicklung des Herrenhemds und dessen Manschette. In Form, Material und Darstellung gingen Manschettenknöpfe immer mit der jeweiligen Mode. Sie wurden und werden von Gold- und Silberschmieden angefertigt, aber auch preiswert hergestellt und in Kaufhäusern angeboten. Besondere Highlights finden sich bei so bedeutenden Juwelieren wie Bulgari, Cartier, Fabergé, Lalique und Tiffany. Sie alle verwendeten auf die Herstellung dieser kleinen Objekte aus Silber, Gold und Platin sowie deren sorgfältige Ausschmückung mit kostbaren Edelsteinen die gleiche Mühe wie bei größeren Schmuckstücken.

Wenn auch manche edlen Stücke ihren Meister heute nicht mehr verraten und wohl für immer anonym bleiben, lassen andere, dank sorgfältiger Punzierung, nicht nur die Edelmetalllegierung erkennen, sondern auch die Werkstätte – in Berlin, London, Moskau, München, Paris, St. Petersburg oder Wien. Die herausragendsten Stücke sind heute meist im Besitz von Sammlern. Nur sehr wenige Manschettenknöpfe haben bislang den Weg in öffentliche Sammlungen und Museen gefunden, obwohl sie in den großen Bereich Mode und Design gehören. Fündig wird man beispielsweise im Bayerischen Nationalmuseum in München, im Germanischen Nationalmuseum in Nürnberg und im Münchner Stadtmuseum, in denen einige Exemplare aus Nachlässen aufbewahrt werden. Eine wirklich bedeutende Sammlung befindet sich im Victoria and Albert Museum in London, kostbare Objekte beherbergt aber auch der Palazzo Zuckermann (Musei Civici agli Eremitani) in Padua.

Im Gegensatz zu anderen kunst- und kulturgeschichtlich interessanten Schmuckstücken existiert über Manschettenknöpfe bislang noch keine deutschsprachige Publikation, in der man sich über die verschiedenen Stilarten, Künstler, Juweliere, Darstellungen und Materialien informieren kann. Anders ist es im englischen, französischen und italienischen Raum, wo dieses Accessoire bereits in der Vergangenheit mehr Beachtung fand. Die Autoren sind deshalb in den vergangenen zwölf Jahren der Geschichte der Manschettenknöpfe nachgegangen. Sie haben nicht nur Firmenarchive und Fachbibliotheken aufgesucht, sondern auch zahlreiche Gespräche mit Sammlern, Antiquitätenhändlern, Gold- und Silberschmieden, Juwelieren, Schmuckfabrikanten und Modeexperten geführt.

Wir möchten allen danken, die mit ihrer Expertise, mit besonderen Objekten, seltenen Entwürfen und Zeichnungen sowie mit wertvollen Hinweisen zur Realisierung dieser Publikation beigetragen haben. Dies sind insbesondere die Münchner Edelstein- und Antikschmuck-Spezialisten Dominik und Rudolf Biehler; der Smaragd- und Diamantexperte Joachim Körber von der FoFo Juwelenbörse, München; Marc G. Stabernack, Juwelier Friedrich, Frankfurt; Gold- und Silberschmiedemeister und Juwelier Maximilian Heiden, München; Goldschmiedemeister Martin Holder, München; Florian Köchert, A. E. Köchert

Precious Cufflinks

Like rings or watches, cufflinks are among the few pieces of jewelry a man could always—and still can—wear unreservedly. Unlike tie pins, which have gone out of style today, these both practical and decorative accessories are still popular and an indispensable item in the world of fashion. Nowadays they can increasingly be found on fashion-conscious women as well, rather than only in the possession of perfectly attired gentlemen, as in the past.

Cufflinks reveal the individual jewelry tastes of their wearers. And they can point to special proclivities and interests. Examples of the latter are cufflinks for car buffs, tennis players, golfers, hunters, anglers, yachtsmen, and horse lovers, as well as for craftsmen's trades, for members of clubs, societies, fraternities, for Rotarians, Lions, Freemasons, and *Schlaraffen*.

The first specimens appeared as early the seventeenth century, yet cufflinks only became common from the late eighteenth century on, as men's shirts and their cuffs evolved. In terms of form, material, and imagery, cufflinks always followed contemporary fashion. They were manufactured by gold- and silversmiths, but also produced inexpensively and sold at department stores. Special highlights are to be found among the range of products of major jewelers such as Bulgari, Cartier, Fabergé, Lalique, and Tiffany. They all spent the same amount of effort on these small objects made of silver, gold, and platinum and their meticulous ornamentation with precious stones as on their large pieces of jewelry.

Even if some precious pieces today no longer reveal the identity of their manufacturer and will likely remain anonymous for ever, others bear meticulous hallmarks that not only identify the particular precious metal alloy, but also the workshop where they were produced in Berlin, London, Moscow, Munich, Paris, St. Petersburg, or Vienna. The outstanding pieces tend to be owned by collectors nowadays. To date only very few cufflinks have found their way into public collections and museums, even though they belong to the major realm of fashion and design. You can find them, for instance, in the Bayerisches Nationalmuseum in Munich, the Germanisches Nationalmuseum in Nuremberg, and in the Munich Stadtmuseum where some specimens from estates are kept. A truly notable collection is at the Victoria and Albert Museum in London, and the Palazzo Zuckermann (Musei Civici agli Eremitani) in Padua, too, holds precious examples.

Unlike other pieces of jewelry of art-historical and cultural-historical import, there are to date no German-language publications on cufflinks in which one can read up on various styles, artists, jewelers, imagery, and materials. The situation is different in the English, French, and Italian-speaking worlds, where this accessory already attracted more attention in the past. Over the past twelve years the authors have therefore examined the history of cufflinks; they not only visited company archives and special libraries, but also talked to collectors, antique dealers, gold- and silversmiths, jewelers, jewelry manufacturers, and fashion experts.

We would like to thank all those who contributed to this publication, be it by making their expertise available, by providing special objects, rare designs and drawings, or by offering valuable suggestions in preparing this volume. They include, in particular, the Munich-based specialists in gemstone and antique jewelry Dominik and Rudolf Biehler; the emerald and diamond expert Joachim Körber of the FoFo jewelry fair in Munich; Marc G. Stabernack of Juwelier Friedrich in Frankfurt; Maximilian Heiden, master gold- and silversmith and jeweler in Munich; Martin Holder, master goldsmith in Munich; Florian Köchert of A.E. Köchert Juweliere in Vienna and Salzburg; Susanne Benz of Münzgalerie in Munich; Ursula Nusser of the Ursula Nusser Auction House in Munich; Robert Hovis of Galerie Rauhenstein—Alter Schmuck in Munich; Hanns Rothmüller, Munich; Dr. Rolf Schenk of Kunstsalon Franke-Schenk in Munich; Michael Scheublein of Scheub-

Juweliere, Wien und Salzburg; Susanne Benz, Münzgalerie München; Ursula Nusser, Auktionshaus Ursula Nusser, München; Robert Hovis, Galerie Rauhenstein – Alter Schmuck, München; Hanns Rothmüller, München; Dr. Rolf Schenk, Kunstsalon Franke-Schenk, München; Michael Scheublein, Scheublein Art & Auktionen, München; Axel Schlapka, Schlapka Kunsthandel, München; Anna-Maria Wager, Wager Antiquitäten – Miniaturen – Alter Schmuck, München; Klaus Menebröcker, Carl Weishaupt in der Galerie P13, München; sowie viele Leihgeber, die ungenannt bleiben möchten.

Die schmuckhistorische Beratung und Autorschaft übernahm dankenswerterweise SKH Dr. Alexander Herzog von Württemberg. Durch ihn gelangten wir an wertvolle Exemplare aus Adelskreisen, denn Manschettenknöpfe wurden einst, wie Krawatten- und Busennadeln sowie Orden und Auszeichnungen, als fürstliche Geschenke für treue Dienste verliehen.

Für die Hilfe bei Recherchearbeiten danken wir Sigrun Rieger von der Bibliothek des Bayerischen Nationalmuseums, München; den Bibliothekaren und Archivaren des Germanischen Nationalmuseums, Nürnberg; sowie der Kunstbibliothek – Staatliche Museen zu Berlin, Lipperheidesche Kostümbibliothek.

Schon bei unserer ersten Publikation über *Kostbare Krawattennadeln* war der Verlagsmanager Dr. Rüdiger Salat durch seine Kontakte sehr hilfreich. Ihm sei ebenso gedankt wie Susanne Wallner, die durch ihre umfangreichen Zuarbeiten, insbesondere zur Literatur über Mode, Schmuck und Manschettenknöpfe, zum Gelingen des Buches beitrug.

Ganz besonderer Dank gilt Thomas Zuhr, dem Geschäftsführer des Hirmer Verlags, der das Projekt von Anfang an unterstützt hat, und dessen Mitarbeitern Rainer Arnold und Hannes Halder. Danken möchten wir auch dem Grafiker des Buches, Rainald Schwarz, für die hervorragende Umsetzung des Themas, und vor allem Gabriele Ebbecke, die uns mit ihrem großen Engagement wie schon bei *Kostbare Krawattennadeln* eine unverzichtbare Hilfe in allen Abläufen des Projektes war.

Die Mehrzahl der Objekte wurde von den Münchner Fotografen Anna-Maria Decker und Marco Struckhoff & Kollege neu aufgenommen. Aufnahmen von wertvollen Fabergé-Manschettenknöpfen stellte uns dankenswerterweise der auf dieses Haus spezialisierte Dr. Alexander von Solodkoff zur Verfügung. Auch den Auktionshäusern Bonhams, Christie's und Sotheby's gebührt unser Dank für die von ihnen gelieferten Fotografien und Informationen.

München, im Dezember 2015

Dr. Walter Grasser   *Franz Hemmerle*

PABLO PICASSO UND SEIN MODELL JACQUELINE ROQUE BEI DEN FILMFESTSPIELEN IN CANNES, MAI 1960

PABLO PICASSO AND HIS MODEL JACQUELINE ROQUE AT THE CANNES FILM FESTIVAL, MAY 1960

lein Art & Auktionen in Munich; Axel Schlapka of Schlapka Kunsthandel in Munich; Anna-Maria Wager of Wager Antiquitäten—Miniaturen—Alter Schmuck in Munich; Klaus Menebröcker of Galerie P13 bei Carl Weishaupt in Munich; as well as numerous lenders who prefer to remain anonymous.

His Royal Highness Dr. Alexander Herzog von Württemberg kindly agreed to contribute to the project both as an advisor and as author on the history of jewelry. Through his intervention we were able to obtain valuable specimens from aristocratic circles, for cufflinks once used to be awarded—like tie and breastpins, as well as orders and honors—as royal bestowments for loyal service.

We are grateful to Sigrun Rieger of the library of the Bayerisches Nationalmuseum in Munich; to the librarians and archivists of the Germanisches Nationalmuseum in Nuremberg; and to the Lipperheide Costume Library at the Kunstbibliothek (Art Library) of the Berlin State Museums for their help with research.

Through his connections, Dr. Rüdiger Salat, publishing manager, was already a great help in preparing our first publication on *Precious Tie Pins*; we are grateful to him as well as to Susanne Wallner, who through her extensive groundwork—especially regarding the literature on fashion, jewelry, and cufflinks—contributed to the success of this book project.

Our special thanks go to Thomas Zuhr, the Managing Director of Hirmer Verlag, who supported the project from the beginning, and to his assistants Rainer Arnold and Hannes Halder. We should also like to thank the graphic artist Rainald Schwarz for his attractive execution of the subject and especially Gabriele Ebbecke for her tremendous commitment—as previously in "Precious Tiepins"—and for her invaluable assistance throughout the entire course of the project.

New photographs of the majority of the objects were taken by Munich-based photographers Anna-Maria Decker and Marco Struckhoff & Colleague. Pictures of valuable Fabergé cufflinks were kindly made available to us by Dr. Alexander von Solodkoff, a specialist for this house. Our thanks are also due to the auction houses Bonhams, Christie's, and Sotheby's for the photographs and information furnished by them.

Munich, December 2015

Dr. Walter Grasser   *Franz Hemmerle*

Walter Grasser

Manschettenknöpfe sind Lebensstil

Über die Entstehung der ersten Manschettenknöpfe ist nicht viel bekannt. Man kann aber davon ausgehen, dass es nicht den »einen« Erfinder gab, sondern dass normale Knöpfe ab einem bestimmten Zeitpunkt eine neue Verwendung fanden. Bis ins 17. Jahrhundert schloss man die Hemdärmel mit Bändern aus Baumwolle, Leinen oder Seide. Um 1650 begannen dann Frankreichs Aristokraten, ihre Ärmel mit »boutons de manchettes« zuzuknöpfen, zunächst mit identischen Paaren farbiger Glasknöpfe, die durch eine kurze Kette miteinander verbunden waren. Während der Regierungszeit Ludwigs XIV. von Frankreich (reg. 1643–1715) waren kostbare Modelle aus Edelmetallen und mit Einlagen aus Perlmutt, Schmuck- oder Edelsteinen beliebt. Auch August der Starke (1670–1733) schätzte wertvolle Edelsteine als Manschettenknöpfe. In der Schatzkammer des Grünen Gewölbes in Dresden befinden sich noch heute zwei große Diamanten, die als von ihm getragene Manschettenknöpfe beschrieben werden. Sie gehören zur berühmten Brillantgarnitur und zählen zu den kostbarsten Stücken weltweit.

Noch bis zum Ende des 18. Jahrhunderts war das Tragen von Schmuck als Symbol der Macht dem Adel und hohen kirchlichen Würdenträgern vorbehalten. Wirklich gebräuchlich wurden Manschettenknöpfe jedoch erst Ende des 19. Jahrhunderts, was eng mit der allgemeinen Entwicklung des Herrenhemds und seines Armabschlusses – der Manschette – zusammenhing. Diese existiert heute in folgenden Typen:

Die *Sportmanschette* ist eine geknöpfte Manschette ohne Umschlag. Die knöpfbaren Teile werden übereinandergelegt.
Die *Kombimanschette* kann sowohl normal geknöpft als auch mit einem Manschettenknopf geschlossen werden.
Die *Umschlagmanschette* heißt auch französische Manschette oder Doppelmanschette. Sie besteht aus einer doppelten Stofflage, die zum Handgelenk zurückgeschlagen und mit einem Manschettenknopf geschlossen wird. Dies ist die eleganteste Form der Manschette und besonders passend zum Abendanzug.

Als Manschettenknopf in seiner einfachsten Form wird ein doppelter farbiger Seidenknoten mit Gummiband verwendet. Manschettenknöpfe können aber aus unterschiedlichsten Materialien bestehen: Diese reichen von Kupfer- und Eisenlegierungen bis hin zu Silber, Gold und Platin. Zur Ausschmückung dienen alle Schmuck- und Edelsteine wie Achat, Lapislazuli, Malachit, Onyx oder Opal, aber natürlich auch Brillanten, Rubine, Saphire und Smaragde, oft in der unfacettierten, runden oder ovalen Schliffform des Cabochons. Es werden aber auch Email, Glas, Stein, Holz und Leder verarbeitet sowie organische Stoffe wie Bernstein, Elfenbein, Horn, Knochen und Korallen. Kombinationen sind keine Grenzen gesetzt, auch Ätzungen und Gravuren können hinzukommen.

Um 1800, als sich die Mode auch dem Bürgertum zu öffnen begann, konnten aufgrund neuer Herstellungstechniken preiswertere Manschettenknöpfe angeboten werden. Sie wurden so zum festen Bestandteil der Herrengarderobe. Für den Mann von Welt, der nun tagsüber einen dunklen Anzug und abends Smoking oder Frack trug, gehörten sie zur gepflegten Erscheinung, und auf dezente Weise konnte er mit ihnen Status und Reichtum demonstrieren.

Ab der Mitte des 19. Jahrhunderts wurde es modern, die Manschette – wie Kragen und Hemdbrust – zu stärken. Dadurch war sie zu steif für die Schließung mit einem normalen Knopf. Dank des industriellen Fortschritts konnten Manschettenknöpfe in Massen hergestellt werden und waren in jeder Preislage verfügbar. So verbreitete sich ihr Gebrauch weiter und damit auch die Vielfalt der Verbundsysteme, von Kettchen zu steifen Verbindern, Stäbchen, Druckknopfmechanik und Doppeleffekt (Knopf oder Manschettenknopf).

Walter Grasser

Cufflinks are a Lifestyle

Not much is known about the origins of the first cufflinks. However, it may be assumed that, rather than there being one particular inventor, regular buttons found a new use from a particular point in time on. Until the seventeenth century, shirt sleeves were closed with bands of cotton, linen, or silk. Around 1650, France's aristocrats then started to button up their sleeves, at first with identical pairs of colored glass buttons that were connected by a short chain. During the reign of Louis XIV of France (r. 1643–1715), sumptuous models of precious metals with mother-of-pearl, jewelry, or gemstone inlays were popular. Augustus II the Strong (1670–1733), Elector of Saxony, likewise appreciated valuable gemstones as cufflinks. Two large diamonds he wore that are described as cufflinks can still be seen today in the Grünes Gewölbe treasury in Dresden; part of the famous brilliant-cut diamond jewelry set, they are among the most valuable pieces in the world.

As late as the end of the eighteenth century, wearing jewelry as a symbol of power was still reserved for the aristocracy and high church dignitaries. It was only by the end of the nineteenth century, however, that cufflinks really became common, associated with the general evolution of the men's shirt and its sleeve ends, the cuffs. Nowadays the following types of cuffs exist:

The *button* or *barrel cuff* is a buttoned cuff that is not folded back. The parts that are to be buttoned are placed one on top of the other.
The *convertible cuff* may be closed with regular buttons or with cufflinks.
The *French*, or *double, cuff* is a fold-back cuff. It consists of a double layer of fabric that is folded back to the wrist and closed with a cufflink. This is the most elegant type of cuff and especially appropriate for dress suits.

The simplest form of cufflink is a double knot of colored silk with an elastic band. Cufflinks, however, can be made of a wide variety of materials, ranging from copper and iron alloys to silver, gold, and platinum. Any gems and precious stones can be used to decorate them, including agate, lapis lazuli, malachite, onyx, or opal, and, of course, brilliants, rubies, sapphires, and emeralds—often in the unfaceted, round or oval shape of the cabochon cut. Enamel, glass, stone, wood, and leather, as well as organic materials such as amber, ivory, horn, bone, and corals may be used as well. In addition to endless combinations of the above, etchings and engravings can also be added.

Around 1800, when fashion began to open up to the middle class, new manufacturing techniques made more inexpensive cufflinks available as well. As a result, cufflinks became an integral part of men's clothing. For the man of the world, who now wore a dark suit during the day and a dress-coat or tuxedo at night, they were part of a well-groomed appearance and allowed him to demonstrate status and wealth discreetly.

From the mid-nineteenth century on it became fashionable to starch the cuff as well as the collar and shirtfront. As a result the cuff was too stiff to be closed with a regular button. Industrial progress made it possible for cufflinks to be mass-produced and to be available in any price range. Thus their usage continued to spread, and with it the variety of interlocking systems from chains to stiff connectors, small rods, snap fasteners, and double effect (button or cufflink).

Colored gemstone cufflinks were initially worn only by self-confident, wealthy men, including trend-setting gentlemen such as the Prince of Wales, later King Edward VII (1841–1910), who towards the end of the nineteenth century popularized the colorful models of Fabergé. Finally, the cufflink developed into a fashionable accessory.

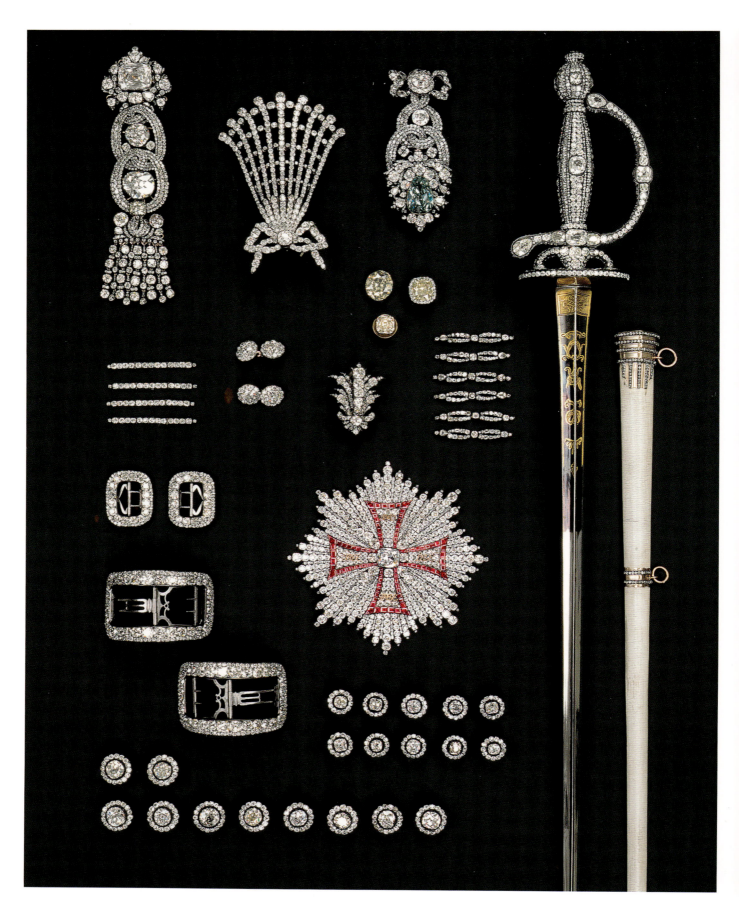

BRILLANTGARNITUR AUGUSTS DES STARKEN MIT BESONDERS WERTVOLLEN MANSCHETTENKNÖPFEN, SIEHE IN DER ZWEITEN REIHE VON OBEN, 1782–1789, HOFJUWELIERE GLOBIG, DRESDEN, STAATLICHE KUNSTSAMMLUNGEN DRESDEN, GRÜNES GEWÖLBE

BRILLIANT-CUT DIAMOND JEWELRY SET OF AUGUSTUS II THE STRONG WITH ESPECIALLY VALUABLE CUFFLINKS, SEE THE SECOND ROW FROM THE TOP, 1782–1789, HOFJUWELIERE GLOBIG, DRESDEN: STAATLICHE KUNSTSAMMLUNGEN DRESDEN, GRÜNES GEWÖLBE

FABERGÉ: CUFFLINKS FOR THE TSAR

Particularly precious specimens came from the workshops of Russian jewelers, especially Peter Carl Fabergé (1846–1920) who carried the title of Imperial Court Jeweler. Nicholas II, the last Tsar (1868–1918), was given valuable jewelry as birthday presents by his parents. On May 2, 1894 he noted in his diary: "… two pairs of beautiful buttons and a divinely beautiful green frog of stone" from Fabergé. Those were his first cufflinks. They are listed in the jewel album he compiled, which was published in 1997 by Fabergé expert Alexander von Solodkoff (see p. 117). It is a unique, authentic documentation of the tsar's extensive cufflink collection. The accompanying illustrations were drawn and painted in watercolors by Nicholas II himself. Included is a pair of cufflinks made of morganite surrounded by a border of diamonds, which he received from Grand Duke Vladimir and his spouse on May 6, 1895.

Cufflinks played an important role for all members of the Russian royal family, who not only wore them, but also liked to give them as presents. Altogether, several hundred specimens have survived, usually still in their original cases from Moscow or St. Petersburg. And their former owners are by and large known, too. Authenticated specimens fetch very high prices in the international trade.

Fabergé's greatest achievement in the eyes of his Paris-based colleagues was the high quality of his transparent enamel. At the 1901 World's Fair his company was able to present various shades of pink, opalescent white and steel-gray, varied hues of blue, yellow, burnt sienna, and dark red.

THEODOR FAHRNER: A PIONEER OF DESIGNER JEWELRY

Theodor Fahrner, Jr. (1859–1919) in Pforzheim was one of the most innovative jewelry manufacturers throughout Europe during the Art Nouveau and Art Deco periods. As early as the end of the nineteenth century he joined the stylistic reform movement and commissioned designs from independent artists in the major artistic centers of Munich, Darmstadt, Stuttgart, and Dresden. At the 1900 Paris World's Fair he presented, among other objects, blued-steel cufflinks with hematite, which had been created by the architect, painter, graphic artist, and designer Max Joseph Gradel. In the first decade of the twentieth century his company thus became a leader in "designer jewelry." After Fahrner's death in 1919, his successor, Gustav Braendle, took over the company and carried on the business under the brand name "Fahrner Jewelry."

The company's jewelry sets include a sizable number of cufflinks, since the latter were in demand as never before in the 1920s. They came in all forms, colors, and materials, both with precious stones and, in inexpensive copies, with glass-cast gems. Also particularly popular at this time were colored enameled cufflinks with geometric patterns: so-called fashion jewelry had become socially acceptable, not least due to trend-setting icons such as Coco Chanel. As a result, there was a great variety of products and always something for every taste and price range. It is therefore not surprising that these small works of art made of precious metal are still sought after by collectors and lovers of jewelry today.

Major centers of production were Idar-Oberstein and Pforzheim. While cufflinks produced in Idar-Oberstein were made of plain materials and for small wallets, the jewelry manufactures in Pforzheim produced models in gold and silver in the mid to upper price segments. Historical and modern-design fine cufflinks are traditionally handcrafted in Pforzheim to this day.

Farbige Manschettenknöpfe aus Edelstein wurden zunächst nur von selbstbewussten, wohlhabenden Männern getragen. Dazu gehörten stilbildende Gentlemen wie der Prince of Wales, der spätere König Eduard VII. (1841–1910), der Ende des 19. Jahrhunderts die bunten Modelle von Fabergé populär machte. Der Manschettenknopf entwickelte sich endgültig zum modischen Accessoire.

Fabergé:
Manschettenknöpfe für den Zaren

Besonders kostbare Exemplare kamen aus russischen Juwelierwerkstätten, vor allem von Peter Carl Fabergé (1846–1920), der den Titel des Kaiserlichen Hofjuweliers trug. Nikolaus II., der letzte Zar (1868–1918), erhielt zu seinen Geburtstagen wertvolle Schmuckgeschenke von seinen Eltern. Am 2. Mai 1894 notierte er in seinem Tagebuch: »… zwei Paar schöne Knöpfe und ein himmlisch schöner grüner Frosch aus Stein« von Fabergé. Dies waren seine ersten Manschettenknöpfe. Sie sind in dem von ihm angelegten Juwelenalbum aufgeführt, das der Fabergé-Spezialist Alexander von Solodkoff 1997 veröffentlichte (siehe S. 117). Es ist eine einmalige, authentische Dokumentation der umfangreichen Manschettenknopfsammlung des Zaren. Die zugehörigen Zeichnungen hat Nikolaus II. selbst angefertigt und aquarelliert. Hier findet sich auch ein Paar Manschettenknöpfe aus Morganit mit Diamantbordüren, das er am 6. Mai 1895 vom Großfürsten Wladimir und dessen Gemahlin erhielt.

Manschettenknöpfe spielten für sämtliche Mitglieder der Zarenfamilie eine große Rolle und wurden von ihnen nicht nur getragen, sondern auch gerne verschenkt. Insgesamt haben sich mehrere Hundert Exemplare erhalten, in der Regel noch in den Originaletuis aus Moskau oder St. Petersburg. Auch die ehemaligen Eigentümer sind weitgehend bekannt. Für authentisierte Exemplare werden heute im internationalen Handel sehr hohe Preise gezahlt.

Fabergés größte Leistung war in den Augen seiner Pariser Kollegen die hohe Qualität seines transparenten Emails. Auf der Weltausstellung von 1901 konnte seine Firma verschiedene Schattierungen von Rosa, opaleszierendem Weiß und Stahlgrau, diverse Töne von Blau, Gelb, gebrannter Siena und Dunkelrot präsentieren.

Theodor Fahrner:
ein Vorreiter des Designerschmucks

Theodor Fahrner jun. (1859–1919) in Pforzheim war zur Zeit des Jugendstils und Art déco einer der innovativsten Schmuckhersteller in ganz Europa. Schon Ende des 19. Jahrhunderts hatte er sich der stilistischen Reformbewegung angeschlossen und freie Künstler aus den wichtigen Kunstzentren München, Darmstadt, Stuttgart und Dresden mit Entwürfen beauftragt. Auf der Weltausstellung in Paris 1900 präsentierte er unter anderem Manschettenknöpfe aus gebläutem Stahl mit Hämatit, die der Architekt, Maler, Grafiker und Designer Max Joseph Gradel geschaffen hatte. So wurde seine Firma im ersten Jahrzehnt des 20. Jahrhunderts führend in »Designerschmuck«. Nach Fahrners Tod 1919 übernahm sein Nachfolger Gustav Braendle den Betrieb und führte ihn unter dem Markenzeichen »Fahrner-Schmuck« weiter.

In den Schmuckgarnituren der Firma befindet sich eine größere Anzahl von Manschettenknöpfen, da diese in den 20er-Jahren gefragt waren wie nie zuvor. Sie wurden in allen Formen, Farben und Materialien angeboten, sowohl mit Edelsteinen als auch in preiswerten Kopien mit Steinen aus Glasguss. Besonders beliebt waren jetzt auch farbig emaillierte mit geometrischen Mustern – der sogenannte Modeschmuck war salonfähig geworden, nicht zuletzt durch stilbildende Ikonen wie Coco Chanel. Das Angebot

DER AMERIKANISCHE KOMPONIST UND DIRIGENT AARON COPLAND, NEW YORK, 1969

THE AMERICAN COMPOSER AND CONDUCTOR AARON COPLAND, NEW YORK, 1969

From the Fifties to the Present

After the Second World War cufflinks were considered antiquated. For a long time the only acceptable men's jewelry aside from the wedding ring was the wristwatch. Only gradually did cufflinks abandon their wallflower existence and rise to become the distinctive feature of an elite that kept alive the traditional style of a gentleman.

Starting in the mid-1950s, things changed, as men adorned themselves with an entire ensemble of cigarette case, lighter, key chain, money clip, and, of course, tie pin and cufflinks. The London scene of the Swinging Sixties generated a new male fashion-consciousness that was epitomized by Carnaby Street dandies such as Mick Jagger. Very fancy cufflinks were now part of an extravagant outfit.

In the course of the 1960s the demand for witty pieces of jewelry became ever greater and each jeweler produced his own variations. The cheerful, colorful pieces of everyday jewelry led *Vogue* and *Harper's Bazaar* to outdo one another with lavish photo series. Among the leading designers was David Webb (1925–1975), "the creative meteor about town," as he was dubbed by the *New Yorker*. His enamel frogs with gold, platinum, diamonds, and rubies were extremely popular and they, of course, came as cufflinks as well.

"He was today's Fabergé"—this assessment by the Duchess of Windsor describes David Webb's status. And, in fact, he admired the jewelry of Fabergé for its sculptural finesse and the ingenious combination of Russian semiprecious stones. He himself liked to use decorative elements of cultures of the past as models. The pieces he de-

DER SÄNGER, SCHAUSPIELER UND ENTERTAINER
FRANK SINATRA, 1950ER-JAHRE
THE SINGER, ACTOR AND ENTERTAINER
FRANK SINATRA, 1950S

war also sehr vielfältig und entsprach jedem Geschmack und jeder Preisklasse. So ist es nicht verwunderlich, dass diese kleinen Kunstwerke aus Edelmetall auch heute noch bei Sammlern und Schmuckliebhabern begehrt sind.

Wichtige Produktionszentren waren Idar-Oberstein und Pforzheim. Während in Idar-Oberstein Manschettenknöpfe aus einfachen Materialien für den schmalen Geldbeutel produziert wurden, stellten die Pforzheimer Schmuckfabriken Modelle in Gold und Silber im mittleren bis gehobenen Preissegment her. In Pforzheim werden bis heute in traditionellem Handwerk edle Manschettenknöpfe in historischen und modernen Designs gefertigt.

Von den Fifties bis heute

Nach dem Zweiten Weltkrieg galten Manschettenknöpfe als antiquiert. Allein zulässiges Herrenschmuckstück war für längere Zeit – neben dem Ehering – die Armbanduhr. Erst allmählich befreiten sie sich aus ihrem Mauerblümchendasein und stiegen zum luxuriösen Erkennungsmerkmal einer Elite auf, die den traditionellen Stil des Gentlemans am Leben hielt.

Anders ab Mitte der 50er-Jahre: Man(n) schmückte sich mit einem ganzen Ensemble aus Zigarettenetui, Feuerzeug, Schlüsselkette, Geldklammer und natürlich auch Krawattennadel und Manschettenknöpfen. Die Londoner Szene der Swinging Sixties brachte ein neues männliches Modebewusstsein hervor, das Carnaby Street Dandys wie Mick Jagger repräsentierten. Sehr ausgefallene Manschettenknöpfe gehörten von nun an zu einem extravaganten Outfit.

Im Verlauf der 60er-Jahre wurde die Nachfrage nach launigen Schmuckstücken immer größer, jeder Juwelier produzierte seine eigenen Varianten. Die fröhlichen, farbigen Tagesschmuckstücke dieser Zeit veranlassten *Vogue* und *Harper's Bazaar*, sich gegenseitig mit üppigen Fotostrecken zu übertrumpfen. Zu den führenden Designern zählte David Webb (1925–1975), »the creative meteor about town«, wie ihn der *New Yorker* nannte. Seine Emailfrösche mit Gold, Platin, Diamanten und Rubinen waren äußerst beliebt, und natürlich gab es sie auch als Manschettenknöpfe.

»He was today's Fabergé.« Diese Einschätzung der Herzogin von Windsor beschreibt den Rang, den David Webb innehatte. In der Tat bewunderte er den Schmuck Fabergés wegen seines bildhauerischen Raffinements und der erfindungsreichen Kombination russischer Halbedelsteine. Er selbst benutzte gern Schmuckelemente vergangener Kulturen als Vorlage. Seine Arbeiten waren kühn und formvollendet und sind dies bis heute. Webb genoss das Vertrauen des Weißen Hauses, und vor allem die Präsidentengattin Jacqueline Kennedy ließ sich von ihm einfallsreiche Geschenke für diplomatische Zwecke liefern.

In den 70er-Jahren des 20. Jahrhunderts verschwanden Manschettenknöpfe fast völlig. Die Woodstock-Generation beherrschte die Mode. Hemden gab es in der Regel nur noch mit Knopflöchern und Knöpfen. Auch nach dem

PRINZESSIN DIANA, FÜRSTIN VON WALES, LONDON, 1989
DIANA, PRINCESS OF WALES, LONDON, 1989

natural part of men's—and women's—fashion ever since. Rather than just with a jacket, they are now often casually combined with a sweater as well, and they are a must-have in combination with elegant business suits, while remaining an obligatory addition to the tuxedo or dress-coat.

Cufflinks: an Ingenious Solution

The shape of cufflinks must follow their function, which makes it easier to survey their basic types. And yet human ingenuity has come up with amazing ideas in this field. A number of patents for special cufflinks existed, for instance, in the German Reich (1871–1918), with inventors securing legal protection especially for the cufflink mechanisms. It was important to some wearers to be able to open and close the cufflinks quickly, and the relevant patent specifications include detailed drawings.

The configuration and decoration of the basic form of the cufflinks, which like earrings appear only in pairs, can take almost infinitely different and often surprising forms. Usually, the same stones are used for both sides. Earrings and cufflinks are frequently interchangeable and sumptuous earrings were often converted into valuable cufflinks.

In order to be able to assess historical specimens, it is important to know by whom and when they were worn. Among European royal houses cufflinks were considered popular court gifts, and, like brooches and tie pins, they were presented to deserving staff members and subjects. The latter understandably cherished them, which is why many such jewelry gifts have survived in their original cases. Pieces such as these are particularly sought after in the art and antiques trade and highly valued—especially those of the renowned jewelers Fabergé, Cartier, Tiffany, and Bulgari. Like other pieces of jewelry, cufflinks were hallmarked and, in case of outstanding pieces, even signed. As a result, their sources can be precisely determined.

signed were—and are—bold and perfectly shaped. Webb enjoyed the trust of the White House, and especially First Lady Jacqueline Kennedy had him provide her with inventive gifts for diplomatic purposes.

In the 1970s cufflinks disappeared almost completely. The Woodstock generation dominated fashion. Shirts now usually just had button holes and buttons. And even after the hippie era few men wore cufflinks. Yet they experienced a renaissance by the end of the 1980s and have remained a

Ende der Hippie-Ära trugen nur wenige Männer Manschettenknöpfe. Erst Ende der 80er-Jahre erlebten sie eine Renaissance und sind bis heute selbstverständlicher Bestandteil der männlichen – wie weiblichen – Garderobe. Gern werden sie auch lässig mit Pullover statt mit Sakko kombiniert. Ein Must-have sind sie in der Kombination mit eleganten Business-Anzügen, und zum Smoking oder Frack bleiben sie die obligatorische Ergänzung.

Manschettenknöpfe: eine patente Lösung

Die Gestalt der Manschettenknöpfe muss ihrer Funktion entsprechen und ist deshalb in ihren Grundtypen überschaubar. Dennoch hat sich der menschliche Erfindungsgeist hier Erstaunliches einfallen lassen. So gab es im Deutschen Kaiserreich (1871–1918) gleich mehrere Patente für besondere Knöpfe, wobei sich die Erfinder vor allem den Mechanismus ihrer Manschettenknöpfe gesetzlich schützen ließen. In den Patentschriften finden sich hierzu genaue Zeichnungen, denn für manche Träger war es wichtig, die Knöpfe rasch öffnen und schließen zu können.

Nahezu endlos und immer wieder überraschend ist die Ausgestaltung und Ausschmückung der Grundform der Manschettenknöpfe, die – wie Ohrringe – nur paarweise auftreten. In der Regel wurden dabei beidseits die gleichen Steine verwendet. Ohrringe und Manschettenknöpfe sind also austauschbar, und so wurden aus kostbaren Ohrringen häufig wertvolle Manschettenknöpfe.

Für die Bewertung historischer Exemplare ist es wichtig zu wissen, von wem und wann sie getragen wurden. Bei europäischen Fürstenhäusern galten Manschettenknöpfe als beliebte Hofgeschenke und wurden, wie Broschen und Krawattennadeln, an verdiente Mitarbeiter und Untertanen verschenkt. Verständlicherweise wurden sie von diesen in Ehren gehalten und haben sich daher häufig in den originalen Etuis erhalten. Solche Stücke sind im Kunst- und Antiquitätenhandel besonders gesucht und hoch bewertet – vor allem die der namhaften Juweliere Fabergé, Cartier, Tiffany und Bulgari. Manschettenknöpfe wurden, wie andere Schmuckstücke, gepunzt und – wenn es sich um herausragende Stücke handelte – auch signiert. So lässt sich ihre Herkunft eindeutig feststellen.

Besondere Bedeutung für die Zuordnung und zeitliche Einordnung kommt den Originaletuis zu. Dies gilt insbesondere für alle Fabergé-Objekte, da sich hier häufig Fälschungen finden.

Manschettenknöpfe werden in jeder Preislage zwischen fünfzig und tausend Euro angeboten, wobei es nach oben keine Grenze gibt. Für wertvolle Exemplare gilt es, einige Tausend Euro zu investieren. Die verwendeten Edelsteine und deren Verarbeitung spielen hierbei eine entscheidende Rolle.

Individuell gefertigte Manschettenknöpfe spiegeln gestern wie heute den Lebensstil und Kunstsinn ihrer Träger wider, etwa die mit Amethyst besetzten, goldenen Manschettenknöpfe von Papst Benedikt XVI. – ein Geschenk des Münchner Domkapitels –, die kostbaren Smaragd-Manschettenknöpfe des Dirigenten Zubin Mehta oder die indischen Kamasutra-Darstellungen eines italienischen Fabrikanten.

Von Albert Einstein ist durch einen Brief vom 26. März 1955 bekannt, dass er noch kurz vor seinem Tod mit Manschettenknöpfen und einer Krawattennadel beschenkt wurde. Die Kinder einer Grundschulklasse hatten ihm damit zum 76. Geburtstag gratuliert. Er bedankte sich mit folgenden Worten: »… Ich danke Euch allen … Euer Geschenk wird mir eine geeignete Anregung sein, in Zukunft etwas eleganter zu sein als bisher …«

DANIEL CRAIG ALIAS JAMES
BOND, MADRID, 2012

DANIEL CRAIG ALIAS JAMES
BOND, MADRID, 2012

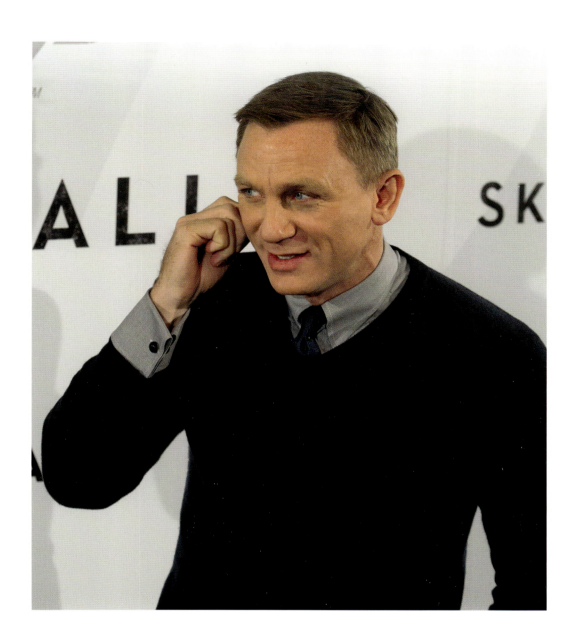

The original cases are particularly important when it comes to classifying and dating the cufflinks. This applies in particular to all Fabergé objects, because here imitations are all too common.

Cufflinks are sold in every price bracket between fifty and one thousand euros, whereby there is no upper limit as regards price. Valuable examples may well cost several thousand euros. The gems used in their manufacture and the workmanship play a decisive role here.

In the past as today, individually manufactured cufflinks reflect the lifestyle and art appreciation of their wearers, as, for instance, the golden cufflinks set with amethyst of Pope Benedict XVI, which were a gift of the Munich cathedral chapter; the precious emerald cufflinks of the conductor Zubin Mehta; or the cufflinks with Kamasutra illustrations of an Italian industrialist. We learn from a letter written by Albert Einstein and dated 26 March 1955, that he received a gift of cufflinks and a tiepin shortly before his death. The children of an American elementary school presented them to him on the occasion of his 76th birthday. He thanked them with the following words: "… I thank you all … Your gift will be an appropriate inspiration to me to look somewhat more elegant in future than I have done in the past …"

Alexander Herzog von Württemberg

Manschettenknöpfe – Schmuck für den Herrn

Arten und Anlässe

Das späte 19. Jahrhundert brachte die Blütezeit der Kultur des Manschettenknopfs. Für Mitglieder des finanziell hinreichend situierten Adels, Diplomaten, höhere Offiziere und Herren der Großindustrie war es üblich, das eine oder andere Paar Manschettenknöpfe von Juwelierqualität zu besitzen. Wenn nicht selbst erworben, waren es in der Mehrzahl Geschenke von Verwandten oder Paten zur Taufe, Konfirmation oder Hochzeit. Damit war ein Grundstock einer standesgemäßen Ausstattung gegeben. Knöpfe aus unedlen Materialien wie zum Beispiel Tombak waren in diesen Kreisen verpönt und galten als unelegant.

Um die Wende vom 19. zum 20. Jahrhundert war es für Herren, die Wert auf ein gepflegtes Äußeres legten und über die entsprechenden Mittel verfügten, gebräuchlich, für abendliche gesellschaftliche Anlässe einen Frack, später einen Smoking, und für offizielle Anlässe am Tage wie Hochzeiten, Taufen oder Beerdigungen einen Cutaway, kurz Cut genannt, zu besitzen. Diese Kleidungsstücke erforderten ein angemessenes Zubehör: beim Frack für die gestärkte Hemdbrust die obligaten Perlen, für die Weste Knöpfe meist aus Perlmutt kombiniert mit Edelsteinen und dazu passende Manschettenknöpfe, farblich aufeinander abgestimmt und zurückhaltend, aber geschmackvoll. Erst mit dem Aufkommen des Smokings als Abendkleidung kamen für die gestärkte Hemdbrust farbige Edelsteinknöpfe und dazu passende Westen- und Manschettenknöpfe gleicher Art in Mode. Zugleich verschwand die Perle aus der Hemdbrust. Besonders in England war die Kultur dieser dreiteiligen Schmucksets reich entwickelt, wobei meist dunkle Granate, Turmaline oder Amethyste Verwendung fanden. Später – und bis heute – wurden diese Sets auch beim Frack übernommen, was das einheitliche Weiß etwas auflockert, aber den ursprünglichen Regeln zuwiderläuft. Herausragende Anlässe erforderten aber auch vornehme goldene Knöpfe mit hochrangigem Edelsteinbesatz, die am Tage wie am Abend Verwendung fanden.

Für den Alltag trug man meist schlichte Knöpfe mit geometrischen Mustern. Gegen Ende des 19. Jahrhunderts bevorzugte man Halbedelsteine aller Art in ovaler oder runder Form, meist als Cabochon geschliffen, in schmaler Goldfassung, bei denen die gleiche Farbe der Steine ausschlaggebend war.

Der elegante Herr trug selbst beim Sport, zum Beispiel beim Tennis, Manschettenknöpfe, die auch als Turnierpreise vergeben wurden. Mit den entsprechenden Emblemen oder Clubabzeichen in Email versehen, fanden hier auch unedle Metalle Verwendung.

Für die gesellschaftlichen Anlässe rund um die Jagd kam im späten 19. Jahrhundert ein eigener Jagdschmuck in Mode, meist in Silber oder Gold gefasste Hirschgrandeln – für die Dame als Brosche, für den Herrn als Manschettenknöpfe oder Krawattennadel verarbeitet. Die hierfür verwendeten Grandeln, bestimmte Eckzähne des Hirschs, die zu den Trophäen zählen und daher dem Schützen zustehen, sollten von selbst erlegten Hirschen stammen und möglichst schlicht verarbeitet sein. Schmuck mit Grandeln von nicht selbst erlegtem Wild, der zu aufwendig verarbeitet war, galt als unwaidmännisch und als schlechter Geschmack. Führend für ansprechend verarbeiteten Jagdschmuck und Jagdabzeichen, meist in patiniertem Silber und kombiniert mit sparsam verwendetem Gold oder Email, waren die darauf spezialisierten Firmen in Österreich, besonders in Wien (Halder), und zum Teil auch in Bayern.

Eine eigene Gattung bildeten die Geschenk- und Gedenk-Manschettenknöpfe, mit denen Monarchen Prominente oder langjährige Verdiente als Zeichen der Anerkennung und Wertschätzung, seltener auch Verwandte als Ausdruck freundschaftlicher Verbundenheit beschenkten (Abb. S. 28). Sie wurden auch nach dem Tod der Könige und Staatsoberhäupter als Erinnerung an diese an ausgewählte Persönlichkeiten und Verwandte geschenkt. Knöpfe

Alexander Herzog von Württemberg

CUFFLINKS: A GENTLEMAN'S JEWELRY

TYPES AND OCCASIONS

The late nineteenth century saw the heyday of the culture of the cufflink. For well-heeled members of the aristocracy, diplomats, senior officers, and businessmen it was common to own one or two pairs of jewelry-grade cufflinks. If not personally acquired, they tended to be baptism, confirmation, or wedding gifts from relatives or sponsors, which thus provided the basis for an accouterment befitting a man's social status. Cuff buttons made of tombac, a brass alloy with high copper content, were frowned upon in these circles and considered unstylish.

Around the turn of the twentieth century it was common for gentlemen who set great store by a well-groomed appearance and had the means to maintain it to possess a tailcoat—later on, a tuxedo—for social evening events and a cutaway, or cut, for formal daytime events such as weddings, baptisms, or funerals. These articles of clothing required proper accessories: in the case of the tailcoat the obligatory beads for the starched shirtfront, for the vest or waistcoat usually buttons of mother-of-pearl combined with gems, and matching cufflinks, color-coordinated and not too conspicuous yet elegant. It was only with the advent of the tuxedo as evening dress that gemstone buttons for the starched shirtfront and matching vest buttons and cufflinks came into vogue. At the same time beads disappeared from the shirtfront. The culture of this three-part jewelry set was particularly refined in England, with dark garnets, tourmalines, or amethysts being most commonly used. Subsequently—and to this day—these sets were adopted for the tuxedo as well, which helps to breaks up the uniform white somewhat, although it violates the original rules. Very special occasions also required exclusive gold cufflinks with high-grade gem settings that were used both in the daytime and in the evening.

For everyday purposes men usually wore plain cuff buttons with geometric patterns. Towards the end of the nineteenth century a preference developed for semi-precious stones of all kinds in oval or round shapes, usually with a cabochon cut and in a slender gold setting, with the identical color of the stones being crucial.

The fashionable gentleman wore cufflinks even when engaging in sports such as tennis. In fact, cuff buttons were awarded as tournament prizes as well. Decorated with the corresponding emblems or club badges in enamel, such buttons could also be made of non-precious metals.

In the late nineteenth century a distinct type of jewelry became fashionable for social occasions related to hunting: it usually consisted of deer teeth set in silver or gold and manufactured into brooches for ladies and into cufflinks or tie pins for gentlemen. The actual teeth used for this were the canines of the deer; considered trophies and therefore the prerogative of the shooter, they were supposed to come from personally bagged deer and were crafted into pieces of simple design. Jewelry featuring canines from deer not personally bagged and too elaborately designed was considered unhuntsmanlike and in bad taste. Leading manufacturers of appealingly crafted hunting jewelry and hunting badges, usually in patinized silver and combined with sparingly used gold or enamel, were specialized companies in Austria, especially in Vienna (Halder), as well as, to some extent, in Bavaria.

Gift and memorial cufflinks formed a separate category and were bestowed on prominent personages or people of long-standing service by monarchs as a token of appreciation and, more rarely, to relatives as an expression of friendship (fig. p. 28). They were also presented to personages and relatives in remembrance of kings or heads of state after their deaths. Cufflinks of this kind usually bore the initials of the reigning or deceased personages. When colored stones were used, the national or dynastic colors were taken into account. Emperor Wilhelm II preferred black and white, the dynastic colors of the Hohenzollern, in enameling.

GESCHENK- BZW. GEDENKKNÖPFE, ZAR BORIS III. VON BULGARIEN (REG. 1918–1943), KYRILLISCHES B UND KRONE, GOLD, DIAMANTROSEN, EMAIL, DEUTSCH (PFORZHEIM?), O.J.

GIFT OR COMMEMORATIVE CUFFLINKS, TSAR BORIS III OF BULGARIA (R. 1918–1943), CYRILLIC LETTER B AND CROWN, GOLD, ROSE-CUT DIAMONDS, ENAMEL. GERMAN (PFORZHEIM?), N.D.

dieser Art waren meist mit den Initialen der regierenden bzw. verstorbenen Persönlichkeiten versehen. Fanden Farbsteine Verwendung, wurden bei diesen die entsprechenden Landes- und Hausfarben der Dynastie berücksichtigt. Kaiser Wilhelm II. bevorzugte bei Emaillierungen Schwarz und Weiß, die Hausfarben der Hohenzollern.

Es konnten auch hohe Geburtstage zum Anlass genommen werden, um den Jubilaren Manschettenknöpfe zu schenken, die mit ihren Lebensdaten verziert waren, wobei die Jahreszahlen über die Knopfpaare verteilt waren (Abb. S. 29 oben). Auch bei Hochzeiten wurden Manschettenknöpfe mit den Wappen oder heraldischen Symbolen der betreffenden Familien an nahe Verwandte und Freunde als Erinnerung verschenkt (Abb. S. 29 unten).

Da nach den Geschmacksregeln des späten 19. Jahrhunderts bei Traueranlässen nur tiefes Schwarz, aber nichts Glänzendes getragen werden durfte, gab es auch hierfür die passenden Manschettenknöpfe, die mit Jett oder Hämatit besetzt waren oder bei denen nur gebläuter Stahl verwendet wurde (Abb. S. 30 links). Dieses Material wurde auch bei Zigarettenetuis verwendet, die während der Trauerzeit benutzt wurden, um anstelle von Gold oder Silber jeglichen Glanz zu vermeiden. Die Strenge der Trauersitten, die vom viktorianischen England ausging, hatte sich in jener Zeit über nahezu alle europäischen Länder ausgebreitet.

Vor dem Ersten Weltkrieg trugen manche Offiziere traditionsreicher Regimenter Manschettenknöpfe, die in Form der Achselstücke des Regiments, in dem sie dienten oder gedient hatten, in Gold und Email gearbeitet waren (Abb. S. 30 rechts oben). Diese Sitte war auch in der Kaiserlich Russischen Armee verbreitet (Abb. S. 30 rechts unten).

Selbst politische Signale konnten von Manschettenknöpfen ausgehen. In der zweiten Hälfte des 19. Jahrhunderts fertigte man in Frankreich aus Goldmünzen der Regierungszeit König Ludwigs XVIII. Manschettenknöpfe, indem man die Münzen möglichst schlicht fasste und durch Knebel verband (Abb. S. 31). Auf diese Weise lugte das Haupt des Bourbonenkönigs aus dem Ärmel hervor und signalisierte jedem Kundigen, wes Geistes der Träger dieser Knöpfe war, sei es als Anhänger der Bourbonen aus der Zeit vor der Juli-Revolution, als Gegner der Bonapartisten oder schlechthin als Monarchist.

Ende des 19. Jahrhunderts wurden auch sogenannte Sankt-Georgs-Taler in Gold mit der Darstellung des heiligen Georg, des Schutzpatrons der Ritterschaft und des Adels, als Manschettenknöpfe gefasst und von Mitgliedern des Adels in Deutschland, Österreich und auch in Russland getragen (Abb. S. 33).

Ein diskreter Blick auf die Manschette und ihren Knopf verriet dem Kenner und Insider, welcher Schicht sein Gegenüber angehörte, ob er einen anspruchsvollen Geschmack hatte und einer bestimmten Gesellschaftsgruppe zuzuordnen war oder ob er sich durch das Tragen von aufdringlichen Knöpfen als Neureicher erwies.

Im Grunde gab es vor dem Ersten Weltkrieg fast keinen Anlass, den man nicht durch Manschettenknöpfe komme-

GESCHENKKNÖPFE, EINEM JUBILAR ZUM 70. GEBURTSTAG (1865–1935) VON ANGEHÖRIGEN GESCHENKT, GOLD, RUBINE, SAPHIRE, DIAMANTEN, DEUTSCH, UM 1935

GIFT CUFFLINKS, PRESENTED TO A JUBILARIAN ON HIS 70TH BIRTHDAY (1865–1935) BY RELATIVES, GOLD, RUBIES, SAPPHIRES, DIAMONDS. GERMAN, C. 1935

OVALE GEDENKKNÖPFE ANLÄSSLICH DER HOCHZEIT VON PRINZ LOUIS VON BOURBON-PARMA UND PRINZESSIN MARIA VON SAVOYEN, ROM 1938, GESCHENK AN ANWESENDE VERWANDTE: DIE HERALDISCHEN LILIEN STEHEN FÜR DAS HAUS BOURBON, DIE KNOTEN FÜR DAS HAUS SAVOYEN. GOLD, SAPHIRE, ITALIENISCH, 1938

OVAL COMMEMORATIVE CUFFLINKS MARKING THE WEDDING OF PRINCE LOUIS OF BOURBON-PARMA AND PRINCESS MARIA OF SAVOY, ROME 1938; GIFT FOR ATTENDING RELATIVES: THE HERALDIC LILIES REPRESENT THE HOUSE OF BOURBON, THE KNOTS THE HOUSE OF SAVOY, GOLD, SAPPHIRES. ITALIAN, 1938

Birthdays in old age could also be taken as an occasion to present the jubilarians with cufflinks featuring their biographical data, with the year dates distributed across the two buttons (fig. p. 29 top). At weddings, too, cufflinks featuring the coats of arms or heraldic symbols of the families involved were presented as souvenirs to close relatives and friends (fig. p. 29 bottom).

Because late nineteenth-century rules of taste for ceremonies of mourning dictated that mourners wear only deep black and nothing shining, appropriate cufflinks set with jet or hematite or made exclusively of blued steel existed for this purpose, too (fig. p. 30 left). The same materials—instead of gold or silver—were also used in cigarette cases reserved for the period of mourning, in order to avoid any shininess. The rigor of mourning etiquette that originated from Victorian England had spread across nearly all European countries at the time.

Before the First World War, some officers of regiments with rich traditions wore cufflinks that were made of gold and enamel in the shape of the epaulets of the particular regiment in which they (had) served (fig. p. 30 top right). This practice was also common in the Imperial Russian Army (fig. p. 30 bottom right).

Cufflinks could also send political signals. In France during the second half of the nineteenth century cufflinks came to be made of gold coins from the reign of King Louis XVIII, using the plainest possible setting and connecting the coins by means of toggles (fig. p. 31). Thus the head of the Bourbon king would peek out from the sleeve and indicate to any well-informed person what convictions the wearer of these cufflinks held, be it as a supporter of the Bourbons from the time before the July Revolution, an opponent of the Bonapartists, or simply a monarchist.

The end of the nineteenth century also saw the emergence of cufflinks made of so-called Saint George thalers: set in gold and featuring depictions of Saint George, the patron saint of knighthood and nobility, these coin cufflinks were worn by members of the aristocracy in Germany, and Austria, as well as in Russia (fig. p. 33).

With a discreet look at a man's cuff and link the connoisseur and insider could tell what social class he belonged to, whether he was a man of discriminating taste who

TRAUERKNÖPFE, ZUM TRAGEN BEI BEERDIGUNGEN UND IN DER TRAUERZEIT, JETT, IN GOLD GEFASST, DEUTSCH ODER ÖSTERREICHISCH, UM 1890–1900

MOURNING CUFFLINKS TO BE WORN AT FUNERALS AND DURING MOURNING, JET IN GOLD SETTING. GERMAN OR AUSTRIAN, C. 1890–1900

OFFIZIERSACHSELSTÜCKE DES KÖNIGLICH-WÜRTTEMBERGISCHEN INFANTERIE-REGIMENTS NR. 121, GOLD, EMAIL, DEUTSCH, UM 1900–1910

EPAULETS OF AN OFFICER OF THE 121ST ROYAL WÜRTTEMBERG INFANTRY REGIMENT, GOLD, ENAMEL. GERMAN, C. 1900–1910

morativ festzuhalten suchte, egal ob Freude oder Trauer, ob Stand oder Beruf – eine vielleicht etwas verspielte Neigung eines Teils der gesellschaftlichen Oberschicht, deren Präsenz mit dem Ende des Ersten Weltkriegs verschwand.

Hersteller- und Stilfragen

Das letzte Drittel des 19. Jahrhunderts war eine Zeit der höchsten Blüte der Goldschmiede- und Juwelierkunst. Die Juweliere spezialisierten sich immer stärker und richteten sich nach den Wünschen und finanziellen Möglichkeiten ihrer Kunden. Auf diese Weise konnten sie für fast jede Gelegenheit das Passende anbieten. Allein in Wien gab es im Jahr 1902 über 800 bei der Genossenschaft eingetragene Gold- und Silberschmiedemeister, die ihre Gewerbeverleihung zwischen ca. 1870 und 1900 erhalten hatten. Ebenso hoch war die Zahl der spezialisierten Zulieferer von Einzelteilen und Sonderaufgaben, die Gold und Silber verarbeiteten und häufig die Galanteriewarenindustrie belieferten.[1]

Inflation und Weltwirtschaftskrise, zuvor der Zusammenbruch der Donaumonarchie nach dem Ende des Ersten Weltkriegs, durch den weite Teile der dortigen Aristokratie verarmten, brachten den Untergang vieler Firmen, denen die Stammkundschaft wegbrach. Zahlreiche Monarchien verschwanden, deren Höfe sichere Auftraggeber waren. Mit einem Mal war es nicht mehr angebracht, die Bezeichnung »Hofjuwelier« zu führen.

Leider sind in vielen Fällen als Folge der beiden Weltkriege, von Flucht und Sorge vor Plünderungen die originalen Etuis der Manschettenknöpfe verloren gegangen, da

OFFIZIERSACHSELSTÜCKE DER KAISERLICH RUSSISCHEN MARINE MIT MONOGRAMM KAISER ALEXANDERS II., GOLD, EMAIL, FABERGÉ, MEISTER ALFRED THIELEMANN, ST. PETERSBURG, 1899–1908

EPAULETS OF AN OFFICER OF THE IMPERIAL RUSSIAN NAVY WITH THE MONOGRAM OF EMPEROR ALEXANDER II, GOLD, ENAMEL. FABERGÉ, MASTER JEWELER ALFRED THIELEMANN, ST. PETERSBURG, 1899–1908

man deren Inhalt auf ein räumliches Minimum zu beschränken suchte. Dadurch ist heute die Herkunft vieler Schmuckstücke nur noch schwerlich zu ermitteln. Manchmal wurden die Etuis auch absichtlich vernichtet, um bei Verfolgungen die Spuren zu verwischen.

Da die meisten Hofjuweliere von einer Stempelpflicht befreit waren, sind zahlreiche Stücke ungemarkt, sodass eine Zuweisung an bestimmte Ateliers und deren Entwerfer äußerst schwierig ist. Nur eine weite Kenntnis vergleichbarer Stücke und langjährige Erfahrung ermöglichen eine ungefähre Zuweisung. Manchmal lässt sich an

VIER GOLDMÜNZEN, KÖNIG LUDWIG XVIII. VON FRANKREICH, ZU JE 20 FRANCS, 1814–1819 BZW. 1814–1824 (TIOLIER/MICHAUT), IN GOLD GEFASST, WOHL FRANZÖSISCH, MITTE 19. JAHRHUNDERT

FOUR 20-FRANC GOLD COINS, KING LOUIS XVIII OF FRANCE, 1814–1819 OR 1814–1824 (TIOLIER/MICHAUT), SET IN GOLD. PROBABLY FRENCH, MID-19TH CENTURY

could be associated with a certain social group, or whether ostentatious cufflinks identified him as an arriviste.

Before the First World War there was basically no event that people did not try to commemorate by means of cufflinks, no matter if joyful or sad and related to class or career—a perhaps somewhat playful penchant of part of the upper class, which lost its presence with the end of the First World War.

Manufacturers and Questions of Style

The last third of the nineteenth century was the absolute heyday of gold work and jewelry. Jewelers increasingly specialized and let the desires and financial means of their customers guide them. In this way they were able to offer appropriate products for virtually every occasion. In 1902 in Vienna alone more than eight hundred master gold- and silversmiths who had received their business licenses between about 1870 and 1900 were registered with the association. Equally high was the number of specialized suppliers of parts and special services who did gold- and silver work and frequently supplied the manufacturers of fancy goods.[1]

Inflation, the world economic crisis, and, prior to that, the collapse of the Danube Monarchy after the end of World War I, which caused large sections of the aristocracy there to fall into poverty, led to the demise of many companies which suddenly lost their regular clientele. Numerous monarchies whose courts had been reliable patrons disappeared. Suddenly it was no longer appropriate to use the title of "court jeweler."

Unfortunately, original cases of cufflinks have in many instances been lost as a result of two world wars, flight and concern about pillages, as circumstances made it crucial for their contents to take up as little space as possible. Thus it has become difficult to determine the origin of many pieces of jewelry. Sometimes cufflink cases were also deliberately destroyed to hide evidence in the case of persecution.

Since most court jewelers were exempted from the obligation to stamp their work, numerous pieces are unmarked, making attributions to particular workshops and their designers extremely difficult. Only a broad knowledge of comparable pieces and many years of experience make an approximate attribution possible. Sometimes a stamp can be discovered in a hidden place that helps, as long as it is not illegible or incomplete. Yet "deciphering" these hallmarks often raises problems, too. Not all control stamps and especially makers' marks are adequately published in the specialized literature by means of images. Imprecise and inconsistent information in this literature can also considerably hamper research.

A selection of exquisite cufflinks of the kind presented here invariably has a certain randomness about it, as it depends on the available pieces that survived the perils of times of war and financial distress. Then again it offers the advantage of a wide range of forms and types. In order to be able to assess the classic jewelry cufflinks that were produced in great variety in nearly all European countries from the mid-nineteenth century on, it is necessary to classify them on the basis of chronological, typological, and stylistic criteria. In the process some groups will also be narrowed down. The mass-produced goods that were—

VIER SOGENANNTE GEORGSTALER, GEDENKMÜNZEN UND INSCHRIFT WIE BEI ABB. S. 46 OBEN, GOLD, TEILWEISE ROT EMAILLIERT, VON DIAMANTROSEN UMGEBEN, FABERGÉ, MEISTER AUGUST FREDERIK HOLLMING, ST. PETERSBURG, 1908–1917
FOUR SO-CALLED ST. GEORGE THALERS, COMMEMORATIVE COINS, AND INSCRIPTION AS IN FIG. ON P. 46 TOP, GOLD, PARTLY RED ENAMELED, SURROUNDED BY ROSE-CUT DIAMONDS. FABERGÉ, MASTER JEWELER AUGUST FREDERIK HOLLMING, ST. PETERSBURG, 1908–1917

verborgener Stelle ein Stempel entdecken, der weiterhilft, wenn er nicht unleserlich oder unvollständig ist. Aber auch die »Dechiffrierung« dieser Punzierungen wirft häufig Probleme auf. Nicht alle Kontrollstempel und vor allem die Meistermarken sind ausreichend in der Fachliteratur durch Abbildungen publiziert. Auch ungenaue und widersprüchliche Angaben in dieser Literatur können die Forschung erheblich erschweren.

Einer Auswahl von Schmuckknöpfen, wie sie hier vorgestellt wird, haftet stets etwas Zufälliges an, da sie von den zur Verfügung stehenden Stücken abhängig ist, die die Fährnisse der vergangenen Kriegs- und finanziellen Notzeiten überstanden haben. Andererseits bietet sie den Vorteil einer breit gefächerten Vielfalt von verschiedenen Formen und Arten. Um die Manschettenknöpfe des klassischen Juwelierschmucks, die seit der Mitte des 19. Jahrhunderts in nahezu allen europäischen Ländern in einer großen Variationsbreite entstanden sind, überschaubar zu machen, ist es erforderlich, sie nach zeitlichen, typologischen und stilistischen Gesichtspunkten zu ordnen. Dabei ergeben sich auch Eingrenzungen. Die Massenware, die in Konfektionsgeschäften zur Vervollständigung der Herrengarderobe angeboten wurde und wird, kann hier nicht einbezogen werden. Auch der zeitgenössische Künstlerschmuck muss ausgeklammert bleiben. Beides würde den Rahmen dieser Studie sprengen, die sich ausschließlich mit dem Juwelierschmuck von der Mitte des 19. bis zum Ende des 20. Jahrhunderts beschäftigt.

Wenn man den europäischen Raum überblickt, lassen sich gegen Ende des 19. Jahrhunderts einige führende Herstellerländer ausmachen: Allen voran England als das klassische Land der Herrenmode mit einer besonders in London hoch entwickelten Juwelierkunst; daneben das Österreich der Donaumonarchie mit einer ungewöhnlichen Dichte an Juwelieren in Wien; dann das deutsche Kaiserreich mit seinen Gliedstaaten und deren großen und kleinen Monarchien, die mit ihren Residenzen bis 1918 bestanden und dort meist recht leistungsfähige Hofjuweliere besaßen, auch wenn diese zu Beginn des 20. Jahrhunderts in zunehmendem Maße als Wiederverkäufer von qualifizierten Lieferanten abhängig wurden.

Bis heute ist dieses weite Feld ungenügend erforscht, vor allem das der meist anonym gebliebenen Zulieferfirmen für den hochrangigen Schmuck in Hanau und für den Schmuck des mittleren Preissegments in Schwäbisch Gmünd und Pforzheim. Ein Desiderat der Forschung sind daher die deutschen Hofjuweliere des 19. und frühen 20. Jahrhunderts, von den großen Hauptstädten wie Berlin, München, Dresden oder Stuttgart bis hin zu den kleinen und kleinsten Residenzstädten wie Weimar oder Coburg. Dazu kommen noch die großen Provinzhauptstädte im Königreich Preußen wie Köln, Koblenz oder Breslau, wo ebenfalls fähige Juweliere ansässig waren, die den Titel »Hofjuwelier« führten.

Es kann hier nicht eine kleine Kunstgeschichte der Manschettenknöpfe ausgebreitet werden, jedoch lassen sich verschiedene Gesichtspunkte herauskristallisieren. Die Formenvielfalt der Schmuckknöpfe wandelte sich nicht so schnell wie die der Kleidermode, aber doch stetig, da die Manschettenknöpfe in gewisser Weise ein – wenn auch etwas teures – Accessoire der Herren waren. Neben Ringen und Krawattennadeln waren sie für den Herrn die einzige Möglichkeit, Schmuck zu zeigen.

Von den großen Stilrichtungen nur gering beeinflusst, entwickelten die Schmuckknöpfe einen relativ eigenständigen Stil, der nationale Varianten einschloss. Man wird vergeblich nach Manschettenknöpfen suchen, die, vom Historismus beeinflusst, gotisierende oder neubarocke Formen zeigen. Im Gegenteil, in der Spätphase dieser Epoche entstand ein Stil, der große, ruhige, geometrische Formen bevorzugte. Der Jugendstil brachte vereinzelt Schmuckknöpfe hervor, die dessen verschlungene Ornamentformen zeigen

and still are—offered in clothing stores to complete men's wardrobes cannot be covered here, and contemporary artistic design jewelry, too, must be excluded. Both would go beyond the scope of this study, which focuses exclusively on classic jewelry cufflinks from the mid-nineteenth to the end of the twentieth century.

When surveying the area of Europe, we can identify a few leading manufacturing countries towards the end of the nineteenth century: first and foremost England as the classic country of men's fashion with a particularly sophisticated jeweler's craft in London; in addition, Austria under the Danube monarchy with an extraordinary density of jewelers in Vienna; then the German Empire with its member states and their minor and major monarchies which existed until 1918, along with their royal capitals where they had for the most part quite capable court jewelers, even if as resellers they became increasingly dependent on qualified suppliers at the beginning of the twentieth century.

To this day this vast area is insufficiently researched—especially the field of the usually anonymous suppliers for high-end jewelry in Hanau and for mid-price jewelry in Schwäbisch Gmünd and Pforzheim. A desirable focus of research would thus be the German court jewelers of the nineteenth and early twentieth centuries, from the major capitals, such as Berlin, Munich, Dresden, and Stuttgart, to the (very) small seats of royal or ducal power, such as Weimar and Coburg. Other centers of the time were the major provincial capitals in Prussia, such as Cologne, Koblenz, and Breslau (modern-day Wroclaw), which were also home to capable jewelers who held the title of "court jeweler."

Even if we cannot present a small art history of cufflinks here, it is possible to identify several aspects. The variety of cufflink forms did not change as rapidly as the fashion in dress, but still did so steadily, since the cufflinks were, in a way, a men's accessory, even if a somewhat expensive one. In addition to rings and tie pins, they were the only means for men to show jewelry.

Only scantily influenced by the major styles, the cufflinks developed a relatively independent style that included national variations. It will be difficult, if not impossible, to find cufflinks that are influenced by historicism and display "Gothicizing" or neo-baroque forms. On the contrary, in the late stage of this period a style emerged that favored large, calm geometric forms. Art Nouveau produced occasional decorative cufflinks that feature its entwined ornamental forms and were frequently set with opal, a popular fashionable stone at the time.

Art Deco was the only style that clearly influenced the design of cufflinks, starting in France with leading jewelers such as Cartier in Paris and, building on these models, in the USA with the major companies in New York. Because the moneyed upper class of the major US cities always wore a tailcoat or tuxedo when visiting the opera or attending evening receptions, the demand for appropriate cufflinks and/or jewelry sets was correspondingly high. Jewelers such as Cartier/New York and Black, Starr and Frost adopted the latest Art Deco styles and frequently arrived at very attractive designs. In a more rigorous, reduced fashion, the leading Italian jewelers in Rome, Milan, and Turin did the same. In Germany the economic crisis of the 1920s left very little room for the development of new styles.

At the same time, from the end of the nineteenth century onward, a timeless variation developed first in England and then predominantly in Germany and Austria, which evolved during the interwar period and flourished again after the Second World War. These are the cufflinks that are defined solely by the round or oval form of an individual gem in a slender setting, with the color intensity being crucial in four-color or, indeed, single-color combinations (figs. p. 34 top and p. 55 top). They were popular with a particular upper-class client base who did not shy away from the bright colors of individual precious or semi-precious stones (figs. p. 35 top and p. 50 top).

VIERFARBIGE KNÖPFE, OVALE CABOCHONS, CITRIN-CHRYSOPRAS BZW. AMETHYST-MONDSTEIN, SEHR SCHMALE GOLDFASSUNG, KETTCHEN-VERBINDUNG, DEUTSCH ODER ÖSTERREICHISCH, UM 1910–1920

FOUR-COLOR CUFFLINKS, OVAL CABOCHONS, CITRINE-CHRYSOPRASE AND AMETHYST-MOONSTONE, VERY SLENDER GOLD SETTING, CHAIN CONNECTION. GERMAN OR AUSTRIAN, C. 1910–1920

und häufig mit dem damals beliebten Modestein Opal besetzt waren.

Erst der Stil des Art déco beeinflusste deutlich die Gestaltung der Manschettenknöpfe, ausgehend von Frankreich, durch die führenden Juweliere wie Cartier in Paris, und diesen folgend in den USA durch die großen Firmen in New York. Da die begüterte Oberschicht der US-Metropolen zum Besuch von Oper und abendlichen Empfängen stets Frack oder Smoking trug, war der Bedarf an edlen Manschettenknöpfen bzw. Schmucksets entsprechend hoch. Juweliere wie Cartier/New York oder Black, Starr and Frost griffen die neuesten Stilformen des Art déco auf und gelangten häufig zu sehr ansprechenden Lösungen. In strenger, reduzierter Form taten dies auch die führenden Juweliere Italiens in Rom, Mailand oder Turin.

In Deutschland ließ die Wirtschaftskrise der 1920er-Jahre der Entwicklung neuer Stilformen nur einen sehr schmalen Spielraum.

Parallel dazu bildete sich seit Ende des 19. Jahrhunderts zunächst in England, dann vorwiegend in Deutschland und Österreich eine zeitlose Variante heraus, die sich zwischen den Weltkriegen weiterentwickelte und nach dem Zweiten Weltkrieg wieder aufblühte. Es sind dies Knöpfe, die allein von der runden oder ovalen Form eines einzelnen Edelsteins in schmaler Goldfassung bestimmt werden, wobei die Farbintensität bei den vierfarbigen oder auch einfarbigen Kombinationen ausschlaggebend war (Abb. S. 35 oben und S. 55 oben). Sie waren bei einer bestimmten gehobenen Kundenschicht beliebt, die keine Scheu vor den leuchtenden Farben der einzelnen Edel- bzw. Halbedelsteine hatte (Abb. oben und S. 50 oben).

Frühe Formen, um 1870–1890

Die frühen Formen der Manschettenknöpfe waren durch die damalige Herrenmode bedingt. Es war die Zeit der hart gestärkten Manschetten, die sich eingerollt um die Handgelenke schmiegten. Das bedurfte großflächiger Knöpfe, meist in geometrischen oder naturalistischen Formen wie Blüten oder Blätter, die mit einem Fuß auf der Unterseite versehen waren, der durch eine Drehbewegung

ZWEI GOLDENE KUGELN, KNEBEL MIT ZWEI KLEINEN KUGELN BESETZT, GOLD, WIEN, UM 1880–1890

TWO GOLDEN SPHERES, TOGGLES SET WITH TWO SMALL BEADS, GOLD. VIENNA, C. 1880–1890

TURMALINE, GROSSE OVALE CABOCHONS, GRÜN BZW. ROT, GOLDFASSUNG, MÜNCHEN, UM 1975

TOURMALINES, LARGE OVAL CABOCHONS, GREEN AND RED RESPECTIVELY, GOLD SETTING. MUNICH, C. 1975

Early Forms, c. 1870–1890

The early forms of cufflinks were contingent on the menswear of the period. It was the era of firmly starched cuffs that, when folded back, fit closely around the wrists. This required large buttons, usually with geometric or naturalistic shapes such as flowers or leaves. They had a foot underneath that was twisted to hold the edges of the cuff together. Numerous examples are featured in the Jewel Album of Tsar Nicholas II, whose uncle, Grand Duke Vladimir, also owned particularly elaborate specimens that were lost for many years but recently auctioned in London.[2]

The complicated detachable cuffs soon went out of fashion and in the early 1880s the large button shapes were initially adopted, reduced in size, and developed into four-part cufflink pairs. The at times rather loud and dandyish shapes were soon abandoned (figs. p. 34 bottom and p. 35 bottom), and the trend very quickly went toward the elegant gold cufflinks that will be discussed in the following section. This development took its course uniformly and, as it spread from London to St. Petersburg and to Vienna, subsequently produced very appealing new forms.

Timelessly Elegant, c. 1890–1910

The two decades before and after the turn of the twentieth century—the Late-Victorian or Wilhelmine period if you will—were the era of heavy gold cufflinks that were set with dark sapphires, sometimes brilliants, and rarely rubies, though hardly ever with emeralds, because their green color was not appropriate for the evening. These cufflinks were suitable for all feasts and formal events such as receptions, weddings, and dinners. Their timeless elegance allowed them to be used on many occasions, except in cases of bereavement.

The major jewelers of the capitals supplied these men's accessories to the ruling houses and the sophisticated clientele of the courts. If they were not their own products, the suppliers usually remained unknown, which compli-

OVALE KNÖPFE MIT MONOGRAMM »A«, FÜR EINEN TRÄGER, DESSEN VORNAME MIT A BEGANN, BLAUES EMAIL AUF GENARBTEM GOLD, KNEBEL GEWIRTELT, AUGUST HAARSTRICK, WIEN, UM 1890–1900

OVAL CUFFLINKS WITH "A" MONOGRAM FOR A WEARER WHOSE FIRST NAME STARTS WITH AN A, BLUE ENAMEL ON PEBBLED GOLD, RINGED TOGGLES. VIENNA: AUGUST HAARSTRICK, VIENNA, C. 1890–1900

OVALE KNÖPFE, DIE AUSSENKANTEN JEWEILS MIT SAPHIREN BZW. BRILLANTEN BESETZT, GOLD, MATTIERT, KEINE MARKEN, DEUTSCH, UM 1890–1900, ORIGINALETUI: EDUARD FOEHR, HOFJUWELIER, STUTTGART

OVAL CUFFLINKS, OUTER EDGES SET WITH SAPPHIRES AND BRILLIANT-CUT DIAMONDS, MATT GOLD, NO MARKS. GERMAN, C. 1890–1900, ORIGINAL CASE: EDUARD FOEHR, COURT JEWELER, STUTTGART

in die andere Hälfte der Manschette eingriff. Das Juwelenalbum des Zaren Nikolaus II. zeigt zahlreiche Modelle davon; ebenso besaß sein Onkel Großfürst Wladimir besonders aufwendige Exemplare, die lange verschollen waren und in jüngerer Zeit in London versteigert wurden.[2]

Da die komplizierten sogenannten Röllchen-Manschetten bald außer Mode kamen, wurden Anfang der 1880er-Jahre zunächst die großen Knopfformen übernommen, in den Ausmaßen verringert und zu vierteiligen Manschettenknopf-Paaren weiterentwickelt. Bald wandte man sich von den manchmal etwas lauten und dandyhaften Formen ab (Abb. S. 34 unten und S. 35 unten), und die Entwicklung ging sehr rasch in Richtung auf die vornehmen Goldknöpfe, die im folgenden Kapitel behandelt werden. Diese Entwicklung nahm einheitlich ihren Lauf, führte von London über St. Petersburg bis Wien und brachte in der Folge sehr ansprechende neue Formen hervor.

Zeitlos vornehm, um 1890–1910

Die beiden Dezennien vor und nach der Wende vom 19. zum 20. Jahrhundert waren die Zeit – man mag sie die spätviktorianische oder wilhelminische nennen – der schweren Goldknöpfe, besetzt mit dunklen Saphiren, wenig Brillanten, selten Rubinen und fast nie mit Smaragden, da deren Grün für den Abend ungeeignet war. Diese Knöpfe waren für alle Festtage und offiziellen Anlässe wie Empfänge, Hochzeiten und Dinners geeignet und in ihrer zeitlosen Vornehmheit bei vielerlei Gelegenheiten, nur nicht bei Trauerfällen, verwendbar.

Die großen Juweliere der Hauptstädte belieferten die regierenden Häuser und die gehobene Kundschaft der Höfe mit diesen männlichen Accessoires. Wenn nicht aus eigener Produktion, blieben die Zulieferer leider meist im Dunkeln, eine Tatsache, die die heutige Forschung erschwert. Die führenden Häuser waren in Berlin Gebrüder Friedländer, in Schwerin Rose, in Kiel Hansen, in Frankfurt am Main Koch, in Dresden Elimeyer, in München Rath und in Stuttgart Foehr, um nur die wichtigsten zu nennen (Abb. oben und S. 51 unten).

Die Grundformen der Knöpfe waren meist oval oder rund, manchmal quadratisch, vereinzelt auch verschlungene Ringe, mit oder ohne Knebel, wobei die Oberfläche teilweise in gehämmerter Technik ausgeführt war. Bevorzugt wurden Saphir und in geringem Maße kleine Brillanten, wie schon angedeutet. Die Verwendung von großen Farbsteinen war eine Frage des Preises, der nicht ausufern sollte, da auch die Budgets der Höfe und der Hofgesellschaft begrenzt waren.

Da die Stücke meist aus 14-karätigem Gold von leicht rötlichem Farbton gefertigt waren, überzog man sie mit einer fein mattierten hochkarätigen Vergoldung, die ihnen ein fabelhaft vornehmes Aussehen verlieh. Dieses Verfahren wurde auch bei Zigarettenetuis angewendet, die dadurch einen intensiven Goldton erhielten und eine höhere Karätigkeit vortäuschten.

Sonderformen für Frack und Smoking

In unmittelbarer zeitlicher Nähe zu der zuvor genannten Gruppe entstanden für spezielle Zwecke – Frack und Smoking – Sonderformen der Manschettenknöpfe und passend dazu auch Hemd- und Westenknöpfe in Juwelierarbeit (Abb. S. 37 unten). Da beim Frack das Weiß der

QUADRATISCHE KNÖPFE, DIAGONAL GETEILT, EINE HÄLFTE GEHÄMMERT, JE EIN KNOPF GOLD, BESETZT MIT EINEM SAPHIR UND EINEM BRILLANTEN, UND EIN KNOPF PLATIN, BESETZT MIT EINEM RUBIN UND EINEM BRILLANTEN, DEUTSCH?, UM 1910–1920

SQUARE CUFFLINKS, DIVIDED DIAGONALLY, ONE HALF HAMMERED; ONE CUFFLINK OF EACH PAIR GOLD SET WITH A SAPPHIRE AND A BRILLIANT, AND THE OTHER CUFFLINK PLATINUM SET WITH A RUBY AND A BRILLIANT-CUT DIAMOND. GERMAN?, C. 1910–1920

cates present-day research. The leading jewelers were Gebrüder Friedländer in Berlin, Rose in Schwerin, Hansen in Kiel, Koch in Frankfurt am Main, Elimeyer in Dresden, Rath in Munich, and Foehr in Stuttgart, to name just the most important ones (figs. p.36 top and p.51 bottom).

The basic shapes of the cufflinks were usually oval or round, sometimes square, and occasionally also intertwined rings, with or without toggle, while the surface sometimes received a hammered finish. As indicated earlier, there was a preference for sapphires and, to a limited extent, small brilliants. The use of large colored stones was a question of price, which was not to get out of hand, as the budgets of the courts and the court society, too, were limited.

Since the pieces were mostly made of 14-carat gold with a slightly reddish hue, they were coated with finely matted high-carat gold plating that lent them a fabulously elegant appearance. The same process was used for cigarette cases as well, which as a result acquired an intense golden color and appeared to be of higher carat value.

SPECIAL TYPES FOR TAILCOATS AND TUXEDOS

Very close in time to the group mentioned above, specific types of jeweler-made cufflinks as well as matching shirt and vest buttons came to be created for special purposes—tailcoat and tuxedo (fig. bottom). Since the tailcoat was dominated by the white of the shirt front and the vest, the preference here was for the lightest colors and plain shapes: for the shirt front only the classic genuine pearl in two or three places; for the tailcoat vest usually mother-of-pearl or rock crystal, set in the center with a small gem; and for the cuffs similar buttons made of white gold or platinum, sometimes set with bright gems or a few small brilliants. Here simplicity was synonymous with elegance.

It was only with the emergence of the tuxedo as evening attire at the beginning of the twenties that colored stones became fashionable for the shirt front and vest buttons and the cufflinks as well. They would come as part of uniformly colored jewelry sets, especially in England, where many

RUNDE KNÖPFE FÜR FRACK ODER SMOKING, AUS AMETHYST GESCHNITTEN, KANTEN FACETTIERT, IN DER MITTE JE EINE PERLE, GOLDFASSUNG, DEUTSCH, ENDFERTIGUNG EVTL. FRANZÖSISCH, UM 1900

ROUND CUFFLINKS FOR DRESS-COAT OR TUXEDO, CUT OUT OF AMETHYST, EDGES FACETED, EACH WITH A PEARL IN THE CENTER, GOLD SETTING. GERMAN, FINISHING POSSIBLY FRENCH, C. 1900

QUADRATISCHE KNÖPFE FÜR DEN FRACK, DICHT BESETZT MIT VERSCHIEDEN GROSSEN DIAMANTROSEN, SILBER AUF GOLD, EINFACHE KNEBEL IN GOLD, UM 1900, GESCHENK DES TÜRKISCHEN SULTANS ABDUL HAMID II.

SQUARE DRESS-COAT CUFFLINKS, DENSELY STUDDED WITH VARIOUS-SIZED ROSE-CUT DIAMONDS, SILVER ON GOLD, PLAIN TOGGLES IN GOLD. C. 1900, GIFT OF THE TURKISH SULTAN ABDUL HAMID II

Hemdbrust und der Weste dominierte, wählte man hier möglichst helle und schlichte Farben und Formen: für die Hemdbrust nur die klassische echte Perle an zwei bis drei Stellen, für die Frackweste meist Perlmutt oder Bergkristall, besetzt in der Mitte mit einem kleinen Edelstein, und für die Manschetten ähnliche Knöpfe aus Weißgold oder Platin, teilweise besetzt mit hellen Edelsteinen oder wenigen kleinen Brillanten. Schlichtheit war hier gleichzusetzen mit Vornehmheit.

Erst mit dem Aufkommen des Smokings als Abendgarderobe zu Beginn der Twenties wurden auch Farbsteine für die Hemdbrust, die Westen- und Manschettenknöpfe Mode und bildeten farblich einheitliche Sets, besonders in England, wo sich viele Modelle, meist ovale Cabochons von dunklen Granaten oder Turmalinen, erhalten haben. Aufwendige Gestaltungen von Manschettenknöpfen waren meist Sonderanfertigungen oder Sonderwünsche der Auftraggeber und bilden eine Ausnahme (Abb. oben).

Exkurs: Russland, um 1890–1914

Ein wichtiges Zentrum der europäischen Juwelierkunst im 19. Jahrhundert war Russland, besonders dessen Hauptstadt St. Petersburg. Der Zarenhof war seit dem Ende des 18. Jahrhunderts der größte und zugleich anspruchsvollste Auftraggeber für hochkarätige Juwelen. Dies traf auch in der Folgezeit auf die für Herren geeigneten Schmuckstücke wie Manschettenknöpfe und Krawattennadeln zu.

Zar Nikolaus II. besaß weit über hundert Paar Manschettenknöpfe. Kein einziges davon hatte er selbst erworben. Er erhielt sie alle als Geschenke von Verwandten und befreundeten Königshäusern zum Geburtstag, zum Namenstag, zur Verlobung, zur Hochzeit, zur Krönung sowie zu Weihnachten und Ostern geschenkt. Der Kaiser hielt in einem penibel geführten privaten Verzeichnis mit eigenhändigen kolorierten Zeichnungen diese Geschenke mit Datum und Namen des Schenkenden fest, leider ohne An-

RUNDE KNÖPFE, GRÜNES EMAIL ÜBER GUILLOCHIERTEM GRUND, IN DER MITTE JE EIN KLEINER BRILLANT, GOLD, FABERGÉ, MEISTER ERIK AUGUST KOLLIN, ST. PETERSBURG, 1899–1908

ROUND CUFFLINKS, GREEN ENAMEL OVER GUILLOCHÉ GROUND, EACH WITH A SMALL BRILLIANT-CUT DIAMOND IN THE CENTER, GOLD. FABERGÉ, MASTER JEWELER ERIK AUGUST KOLLIN, ST. PETERSBURG, 1899–1908

SPITZOVALE KNÖPFE, RUSSISCHE KAISERKRONE BZW. FLORALES ORNAMENT, GOLD, WEISSES EMAIL, DIE KRONEN MIT SAPHIREN BESETZT, FABERGÉ, MEISTER AUGUST FREDERIK HOLLMING, ST. PETERSBURG, 1899–1908

POINTED OVAL CUFFLINKS, RUSSIAN IMPERIAL CROWN AND FLORAL ORNAMENT RESPECTIVELY, GOLD, WHITE ENAMEL, CROWNS SET WITH SAPPHIRES. FABERGÉ, MASTER JEWELER AUGUST FREDERIK HOLLMING, ST. PETERSBURG, 1899–1908

specimens, usually oval cabochons of dark garnets or tourmalines, have survived. Elaborately designed cufflinks which were usually custom-made or specially requested by clients are an exception (fig. p. 38 top).

Digression: Russia, c. 1890–1914

A major center of European jewelry in the nineteenth century was Russia, especially its capital, St. Petersburg. Since the late eighteenth century, the tsar's court was the principal and, at the same time, most demanding commissioner of high-quality jewelry. Later on, this was also true for the pieces of jewelry that were appropriate for men, such as cufflinks and tie pins.

Tsar Nicholas II owned well over one hundred pairs of cufflinks, not one of which he had acquired himself. He received them all as gifts from relatives and friendly royal houses for his birthday, name day, engagement, wedding, coronation, as well as for Christmas and Easter. The emperor recorded these gifts, with the date and name of the giver, in a meticulously kept private catalogue featuring colored drawings by his own hand. Regrettably, he did not include information on the precious stones, let alone on the particular jewelers. All that mattered to him was the occasion and the identity of the giver. Fortunately, this catalogue has survived in the Kremlin Museums in Moscow and in 1977 it was for the first published in its entirety.[3] Covering the period from 1879 until 1913, it includes 305 pieces of jewelry, all of which are sadly lost today.

The drawings allow us to trace the formal and stylistic development of the cufflinks during the period under discussion: from the large single-piece cufflinks for detachable cuffs, which had a foot on the back and were inserted into the firmly starched cuffs by twisting them, to the two-part buttons with toggles of the following period through to the four-part links with identical or almost identical designs for the turnback cuffs of the late years (fig. p. 38 bottom). Only the large links for detachable cuffs disappeared soon after 1890, while attractive types of two- and four-part cufflinks developed very quickly (fig. above). Around 1900, Art Nouveau-influenced cufflink types sporadically appeared, albeit only on a small scale, because the taste of the aristocratic upper-class was less partial to contemporary art than that of the bourgeoisie at the time—a development that similarly manifested itself in Imperial Vienna during this period.

One would have wished that other monarchs, such as the emperors Franz Joseph and Wilhelm II or the kings of Saxony, Bavaria, and Württemberg, had compiled similar jewelry records to that of Nicholas II during this period. Many dating issues would be significantly easier to solve today. But the prosaic taste of the Austrian emperor was disinclined to this, as was that of Wilhelm II who was more interested in things military. The last kings of Saxony and Bavaria were modest and austere in their lifestyles and had little interest in such pursuits. Only Queen Mary of England had a keen interest in jewelry, which she managed to wear in an unequivocally majestic manner. She had precise photograph albums of her jewelry compiled that to this day, unfortunately, have not been published.

In Russia Fabergé was the leading jewelry house for all gifts of the emperor and the imperial family, but aside from that there were other highly productive jewelers as well who, in some cases, were also purveyors to the court, such as Bolin, Hahn, and Köchli, to mention only a few. Here,

VIERFARBIGE KNÖPFE, OVAL, SOGENANNTER MADEIRA-TOPAS (CITRIN), TURMALIN, CITRIN, AMETHYST, OBERFLÄCHE SCHWACH GEWÖLBT, UNTERSEITE FACETTIERT, SCHMALE GOLDFASSUNG, ZUSÄTZLICH WEISSER EMAILRAND, DEUTSCH, UM 1900–1920

FOUR-COLOR CUFFLINKS, OVAL, SO-CALLED MADEIRA TOPAZ (CITRINE), TOURMALINE, CITRINE, AMETHYST, SURFACE SLIGHTLY CURVED, FACETED AT THE BOTTOM, SLENDER GOLD SETTING, ADDITIONAL WHITE ENAMEL RIM. GERMAN, C. 1900–1920

gaben zu den Edelsteinen, geschweige denn einer Erwähnung der betreffenden Juweliere. Wichtig war für ihn allein der Anlass und die Person des Schenkenden. Glücklicherweise hat sich dieses Verzeichnis im Staatlichen Kreml-Museum in Moskau erhalten und wurde im Jahr 1977 zum ersten Mal vollständig veröffentlicht.[3] Es umfasst den Zeitraum von 1879 bis 1913 und enthält 305 Schmuckstücke, die heute leider alle verschollen sind.

Die formale und stilistische Entwicklung der Schmuckknöpfe in jener Zeit lässt sich an diesen Zeichnungen gut ablesen: von den großformatigen einteiligen Knöpfen für die sogenannten Röllchen-Manschetten, die durch einen auf der Rückseite angebrachten Fuß durch eine Drehbewegung in die hart gestärkten Manschetten eingeführt wurden, über die zweiteiligen, mit Knebel versehenen Knöpfe der Folgezeit bis zu den vierteiligen Knöpfen in gleicher oder nahezu gleicher Gestaltung für die Umlegemanschetten der Spätzeit (Abb. S. 38 unten). Lediglich die großformatigen Knöpfe für die Röllchen-Manschetten verschwanden bald nach 1890, während sich sehr rasch äußerst ansprechende Formen von zwei- und vierteiligen Schmuckknöpfen entwickelten (Abb. S. 39 oben). Um 1900 tauchten vereinzelt vom Jugendstil beeinflusste Formen auf, aber nur in geringem Umfang, da der Geschmack der aristokratischen Oberschicht weniger der zeitgenössischen Kunst zugetan war als der des Großbürgertums in jener Zeit. Eine Entwicklung, die sich in gleicher Weise auch im kaiserlichen Wien dieser Zeit abzeichnete.

Man wünschte, andere Monarchen wie die Kaiser Franz Joseph und Wilhelm II. oder die Könige von Sachsen, Bayern und Württemberg hätten in dieser Zeit solch genaue Schmuckverzeichnisse angelegt wie Nikolaus II. Viele Datierungsfragen wären heute wesentlich einfacher zu lösen. Aber der trockene Geschmack des österreichischen Kaisers war diesen Dingen nicht zugeneigt, ebenso wenig wie der Wilhelms II., den Militärisches mehr interessierte. Die letzten Könige von Sachsen und Bayern waren von bescheidener und nüchterner Lebensweise und hatten wenig Interesse an solchen Beschäftigungen. Lediglich Queen Mary von Großbritannien besaß ein ausgeprägtes Interesse an Schmuck, den sie in geradezu majestätischer Weise zu tragen wusste. Von ihrem Schmuck ließ sie genaue Fotoalben anlegen, die leider bis heute nicht veröffentlicht wurden.

In Russland war das Haus Fabergé führend bei allen Geschenken des Kaisers und des Kaiserhauses, aber daneben gab es auch andere leistungsstarke Juweliere, die zum Teil auch Hoflieferanten waren wie Bolin, Hahn oder Köchli, um nur einige wenige zu nennen. Auch hier ist eine Parallele zu Wien in dieser Zeit zu sehen, wo A. E. Köchert führend bei allen Geschenken des Kaisers und des Erzhauses war, daneben aber eine Vielzahl sehr fähiger Juweliere tätig war, die hochkarätigen Schmuck anfertigten. Die Schmuckgeschenke des englischen Königshauses stammten von den Hofjuwelieren Garrard und Collingwood in London.

SPIEL DER FARBEN, 1900 BIS HEUTE

Nie kam die farbliche Pracht der Edelsteine besser zur Geltung als bei den vierfarbigen Knöpfen, die im ersten Viertel des 20. Jahrhunderts entstanden und sich im Lauf des ganzen Jahrhunderts stetig weiterentwickelten. Jeder Knopf bestand nur aus einem runden oder ovalen Cabochon in schmaler Goldfassung, aber das Geschick der

TIEFDUNKLE AMETHYSTE, OVAL, OBERFLÄCHE SCHWACH GEWÖLBT, UNTERSEITE FACETTIERT, SCHMALE GOLDFASSUNG, WOHL DEUTSCH, UM 1900–1920

DEEP DARK AMETHYSTS, OVAL, SURFACE SLIGHTLY CURVED, FACETED AT THE BOTTOM, SLENDER GOLD SETTING. PROBABLY GERMAN, C. 1900–1920

TIEFDUNKLE AMETHYSTE, SCHMALE, HOHE CABOCHONS, SCHMALE GOLDFASSUNG, ZUSÄTZLICH WEISSER EMAILRAND, DEUTSCH, UM 1900–1920, ORIGINALETUI: F. MILLER SOHN, ULM A.D., DONAUSTRASSE 1

DEEP DARK AMETHYSTS, SLENDER HIGH CABOCHONS, SLENDER GOLD SETTING, ADDITIONAL WHITE ENAMEL RIM. GERMAN, C. 1900–1920, ORIGINAL CASE: F. MILLER SOHN, ULM, DONAUSTRASSE 1

VIERFARBIGE KNÖPFE, RUND, MONDSTEIN, SOGENANNTER MADEIRA-TOPAS, CITRIN, AMETHYST, OBERFLÄCHE SCHWACH GEWÖLBT, UNTERSEITE FACETTIERT, GOLD, DEUTSCH, UM 1900–1920

FOUR-COLOR CUFFLINKS, ROUND, MOONSTONE, SO-CALLED MADEIRA TOPAZ, CITRINE, AMETHYST, SURFACE SLIGHTLY CURVED, FACETED AT THE BOTTOM, GOLD. GERMAN, C. 1900–1920

again, we can see a parallel to contemporary Vienna where A.E. Köchert was the foremost purveyor of gifts of the emperor and the archducal house, while a large number of other very capable jewelers who manufactured high-quality jewelry were active there as well. The jewelry gifts of the English royal house came from the court jewelers Garrard and Collingwood in London.

RUBINE, OVALE CABOCHONS, BREITE GOLDFASSUNG,
SCHLICHTE KNEBEL IN GOLD, BLEIHOLDER, MÜNCHEN,
UM 1970–1975
RUBIES, OVAL CABOCHONS, WIDE GOLD SETTING, PLAIN
TOGGLES IN GOLD. BLEIHOLDER, MUNICH, C. 1970–1975

Schleifer ließ diese Steine ihre volle Leuchtkraft ungehemmt entfalten.

Die Herren griffen bei dieser neuen Art von Knöpfen gerne zu, zumal diese den Vorteil hatten, wesentlich preisgünstiger zu sein als die schweren Goldknöpfe, die ehedem in Mode waren. Die neuen Knöpfe ließen sich zu jedem Anlass, außer zum Frack, tragen und erregten die Beachtung, wenn nicht sogar Neugier der anderen Herren. Sie wurden schlechthin zum »Hingucker« der neuen Zeit und zum Gradmesser des guten Geschmacks ihrer Träger. Allzu groß oder allzu laut in den Farben, verrieten sie den schlechten Geschmack des Trägers oder dessen sozialen Aufstieg als Neureicher.

Der Beginn dieser neuen Knopfart setzte um die Wende zum 20. Jahrhundert mit sehr kleinen Cabochons gleicher Steinart ein (vgl. Abb. S. 50 oben). Langsam gewannen die Eigenheit und Farbkraft der Edelsteine die Oberhand, und im Lauf der folgenden Jahre entwickelten sich größere Formen und neue Farbkombinationen, die manchmal von erstaunlicher Vielfalt waren (Abb. S. 35 oben). Auch erfand man trickreiche Konstruktionen durch unsichtbare oder zusätzliche emaillierte Fassungen, die wie ein Rahmen die Edelsteine umfassten und ihre Farbkraft erhöhten (Abb. S. 40 und S. 48 unten). Dazu wurden sehr bald raffinierte Schliffformen entwickelt, bei denen die Oberfläche der Steine nur sehr gering gewölbt, der untere Teil aber mit Facetten ähnlich wie bei einem Brillanten versehen war. Das durch die Facetten reflektierende Licht verstärkt die Leuchtkraft der Edelsteine und hebt die Eigenfarbigkeit der Steine deutlich hervor (Abb. S. 41 oben und unten). Wann und wo diese neue Schliffform entwickelt wurde, liegt noch im unerforschten Dunkel. Findigen Schleifern in Idar-Oberstein ist sie jedenfalls zuzutrauen.

Die Zeit nach dem Zweiten Weltkrieg brachte eine neue Entwicklung bei der Gestaltung von Manschettenknöpfen. Nun standen sowohl das Steinmaterial als auch die ihm eigene Farbe im Mittelpunkt der Komposition. Auf Fassungen in Gold oder Silber wurde verzichtet. Die Knöpfe wurden in ihrer Ganzheit aus Edelsteinen geschnitten, meist in runder, flacher oder kugeliger Form, mit oder ohne Knebel aus dem gleichen Material oder auch in verkleinerter Form für die Innenseite der Manschette. Dazu wurden farbige Akzente in der Mitte der Knöpfe angebracht durch sehr kleine, in Gold gefasste Edelsteine wie Rubine, Saphire oder Smaragde, die den Knöpfen eine farblich äußerst kontrastreiche Höhung verliehen (Abb. S. 112 und 113). Ansätze in Richtung dieser neuen Form hatte es schon um die Wende vom 19. zum 20. Jahrhundert gegeben, als bei Frackgarnituren die Knöpfe aus facettierten Bergkristallen oder Amethysten gebildet wurden, die in der Mitte durch eine Perle oder einen Edelstein gehöht waren (Abb. S. 37 unten). Besonderer Beliebtheit erfreuten sich diese modernen farbigen Steinknöpfe in Italien (Fa. Villa, Mailand), aber auch in Norddeutschland, wobei hier die Frage nach dem Hersteller offenbleiben muss.

Daneben bestehen bis heute die klassischen, in Gold gefassten Rund- oder Ovalformen von Knöpfen mit schlichtem Knebel, aber besetzt mit leuchtenden Cabochons von Rubinen und Saphiren, die eine gediegene Vornehmheit ausstrahlen (Abb. oben und S. 43).

1 Vgl. Verzeichnis der Mitglieder der Genossenschaft der Juweliere, Gold- und Silberschmiede der k. k. Reichshaupt- und Residenzstadt Wien 1902, S. 34–56 und 61–72.
2 *Romanov Heirlooms. The Lost Inheritance of Grand Duchess Maria Pavlovna.* Katalog Auktionshaus Sotheby's, London, 20. November 2008.
3 Alexander von Solodkoff, *The Jewel Album of Tsar Nicholas II and A Collection of Private Photographs of the Russian Imperial Family.* With an Essay by Irina A. Bogatskaya, Curator of the Archives at the State Museums of the Moscow Kremlin, London 1997.

SAPHIRE, OVALE CABOCHONS, BREITE GOLDFASSUNG,
SCHLICHTE KNEBEL, BLEIHOLDER, MÜNCHEN, UM 1990–2000

SAPPHIRES, OVAL CABOCHONS, WIDE GOLD SETTING, PLAIN
TOGGLES. BLEIHOLDER, MUNICH, C. 1990–2000

Play of Colors, 1900 to the Present

The colorfulness of the precious stones is never more magnificent than in the four-color cufflinks that were created in the first quarter of the twentieth century and that continued to develop throughout the century. Each cufflink consisted merely of a round or oval cabochon in a slender gold setting, yet the skill of the cutters allowed these stones to unfold their full vibrancy uninhibitedly.

Gentlemen were happy to acquire cufflinks of this new type, especially since they had the advantage of being considerably cheaper than the heavy gold cufflinks that were previously fashionable. The new cufflinks could be worn on any occasion, just not with a tailcoat, and attracted the attention, if not the curiosity, of other gentlemen. They became the epitome of the modern-day "eye-catcher" and a gauge of good taste. If too big or their colors too loud, they were indicative of their wearer's bad taste or social advancement as a nouveau riche.

The first incarnation of this new type of cufflink, which appeared around the turn of the twentieth century, was characterized by very small cabochons of one and the same kind of stone (cf. fig. p. 50 bottom). Gradually, the peculiarity and color intensity of the precious stones prevailed and in the following years large forms and new color combinations developed which sometimes showed an astonishing diversity (fig. p. 35 top). Jewelers also came up with clever designs featuring invisible or additional enameled settings that surrounded the gems like a frame and enhanced their color intensity (figs. p. 40 and p. 48 bottom). Also, it was not long before very subtle cuts were developed that left the surface of the stones just slightly curved, while the lower part was faceted similar to a brilliant. The light reflected by the facets enhances a gem's brilliance and clearly accentuated its natural color (fig. p. 41 top and bottom). The question as to when and where this new type of cut was developed remains unexplored and unresolved; resourceful cutters in Idar-Oberstein would surely have been capable of it.

The period after the Second World War brought a new development in the design of cufflinks. Now both the stone material and its natural color were central to the composition. Settings and gold or silver were eschewed. The cuff buttons were cut from precious stones as a whole, usually in a round, flat, or spherical shape and with or without a toggle made from the same material—or, indeed, in a reduced form for the inside of the cuff. In addition, small gems set in gold, such as rubies, sapphires, or emeralds, were placed in the middle of the buttons to create color accents that lent the buttons extreme color-contrasted highlights (figs. pp. 112 and 113). First steps in this direction had already been taken around the turn of the twentieth century when the cufflinks in tailcoat sets were made out of faceted rock crystals or amethysts that were heightened with a pearl or a precious stone in the middle (fig. p. 37 bottom). These modern stone buttons were particularly popular in Italy (the Villa company in Milan), but also in northern Germany, though a manufacturer there has not yet been identified.

Aside from this there are, to this day, the classic gold-mounted rounded or oval-shaped cufflinks that have a plain toggle, yet are set with shining cabochons of rubies and sapphires which exude dignified elegance (figs. p. 42 and above).

1. See the register of members of the Association of Jewelers, Gold- and Silversmiths of the Imperial-Royal Capital City of Vienna 1902, pp. 34–56 and 61–72.
2. *Romanov Heirlooms. The Lost Inheritance of Grand Duchess Maria Pavlovna.* Catalogue of the Sotheby's auction house, London, 20 November 2008.
3. Alexander von Solodkoff, *The Jewel Album of Tsar Nicholas II and A Collection of Private Photographs of the Russian Imperial Family.* With an essay by Irina A. Bogatskaya, Curator of the Archives at the State Museums of the Moscow Kremlin (London: Ermitage, 1997).

Kostbare Manschettenknöpfe
vom Ende des 19. Jahrhunderts bis heute

Precious Cufflinks from the End
of the 19th Century to the Present Day

1880–1919

1920–1939

1940–1959

1960–1979

1980–2015

RUNDE METALLKNÖPFE MIT KETTCHEN-VERBINDUNG, (STARKE TRAGESPUREN), BLAUE GLASSTEINE, VOR 1900

ROUND METAL CUFFLINKS WITH CHAIN CONNECTION (PRONOUNCED SIGNS OF WEAR), BLUE GLASS STONES, BEFORE 1900

ZWEI LAPIS-KUGELN, KNEBEL MIT ZWEI KLEINEN LAPIS-KUGELN BESETZT, GOLD, LAPISLAZULI, WIEN, UM 1880–1890

TWO LAPIS BALLS, TOGGLES SET WITH TWO SMALL LAPIS BEADS, GOLD, LAPIS LAZULI. VIENNA, C. 1880–1890

VIER SOGENANNTE GEORGSTALER, GEDENKMÜNZEN MIT INSCHRIFT: ST. GEORGIUS EQUITUM PATRONUS (HEILIGER GEORG SCHUTZPATRON DES RITTERTUMS UND DES ADELS), MEDAILLONS GOLD, IN GOLD GEFASST, SÜDDEUTSCH, ENDE 19. JAHRHUNDERT

FOUR SO-CALLED ST. GEORGE THALERS, COMMEMORATIVE COINS WITH INSCRIPTION: ST. GEORGIUS EQUITC. PATRONUS (ST. GEORGE PATRON SAINT OF KNIGHTHOOD AND NOBILITY), MEDALLIONS GOLD, SET IN GOLD. SOUTHERN GERMAN, END 19TH CENTURY

FLACHE RUNDKNÖPFE, IN DER MITTE JE EIN SAPHIR, KNEBEL SPITZOVAL, GOLD, MATTIERT, MEISTERMARKE UNVOLLSTÄNDIG, WIEN, UM 1890–1900

FLAT ROUND CUFFLINKS, EACH WITH A SAPPHIRE IN THE CENTER, POINTED OVAL TOGGLES, MATT GOLD, MAKER'S MARK INCOMPLETE. VIENNA, C. 1890–1900

ORNAMENTALE KNÖPFE, GOLD, JEWEILS MIT OVALEM SAPHIR-CABOCHON BESETZT, FRIEDRICH KOECHLI, ST. PETERSBURG, 1899–1908

ORNAMENTAL CUFFLINKS, GOLD, EACH SET WITH AN OVAL SAPPHIRE CABOCHON. FRIEDRICH KOECHLI, ST. PETERSBURG, 1899–1908

KAISERLICH RUSSISCHE GESCHENKKNÖPFE FÜR KÜNSTLER DES EREMITAGE-THEATERS, SPITZOVAL MIT EINFACHEN KNEBELN, DER AN DER LINKEN SEITE UNTERBROCHENE GOLDRAND UND DER QUERBALKEN UNTER DER KAISERKRONE BILDEN DAS KYRILLISCHE »E«, KRONE ÜBER ROTEM GUILLOCHIERTEM EMAILGRUND UND KNEBEL BESETZT MIT DIAMANTROSEN, FABERGÉ, MEISTER AUGUST FREDERIK HOLLMING, ST. PETERSBURG, 1899–1908

RUSSIAN IMPERIAL GIFT CUFFLINKS FOR ARTISTS OF THE HERMITAGE THEATER, POINTED OVAL WITH PLAIN TOGGLES, THE GOLD RIM INTERRUPTED ON THE LEFT SIDE AND THE CROSSBAR UNDERNEATH THE IMPERIAL CROWN FORM THE CYRILLIC LETTER "E", CROWN OVER RED GUILLOCHÉ ENAMEL GROUND AND TOGGLES SET WITH ROSE-CUT DIAMONDS. FABERGÉ, MASTER JEWELER AUGUST FREDERIK HOLLMING, ST. PETERSBURG, 1899–1908

KNÖPFE FÜR DEN FRACK, GROSSE OVALE ZIRKONE, CABOCHONS, BLAUGRÜN BZW. HONIGFARBEN, MIT BRILLANTEN AUSGEFASST, DIE KNEBEL AN DEN ENDEN MIT PERLEN BESETZT, GOLDFASSUNG, UM 1890–1900, ORIGINALETUI: ZINSER, KGL. HOFJUWELIER, STUTTGART, AUS DEM PRIVATBESITZ VON KÖNIG WILHELM II. VON WÜRTTEMBERG

DRESS-COAT CUFFLINKS, LARGE OVAL ZIRCONS, CABOCHONS, BLUE-GREEN AND HONEY-COLORED RESPECTIVELY, PAVED WITH BRILLIANT-CUT DIAMONDS, TOGGLES SET WITH PEARLS AT THE ENDS, GOLD SETTING. C. 1890–1900, ORIGINAL CASE: ZINSER, COURT JEWELER, STUTTGART, FROM THE PRIVATE COLLECTION OF KING WILLIAM II OF WÜRTTEMBERG

FRACKGARNITUR, BESTEHEND AUS EINEM PAAR MANSCHETTEN- UND DREI HEMDKNÖPFEN, GOLD, SMARAGDE, PERLMUTT, WOHL FRANKREICH, UM 1910

DRESS-COAT JEWELRY SET CONSISTING OF A PAIR OF CUFFLINKS AND THREE SHIRT STUDS, GOLD, EMERALDS, MOTHER-OF-PEARL. PROBABLY FRANCE, C. 1910

BRAUNE BANDACHATE, HALBKUGELN, GOLDFASSUNG NUR IN SEITENANSICHT ERKENNBAR, FRANZÖSISCH?, UM 1900–1910

BROWN BANDED AGATES, SEMI-SPHERES, GOLD SETTING VISIBLE ONLY FROM THE SIDE. FRENCH?, C. 1900–1910

ZIERLICHE RUNDE KNÖPFE,
GOLD, SILBER, DIAMANTROSEN,
TÜRKISE, FRANKREICH,
UM 1880–1890

DELICATE ROUND BUTTON
CUFFLINKS, GOLD, SILVER,
DIAMOND ROSES, TURQUOISES.
FRANCE, C. 1880–1890

KLEINE DUNKLE AMETHYSTE, OVALE CABOCHONS, SCHMALE KASTENFASSUNG, GOLD, MARKEN UNVOLLSTÄNDIG, WOHL FRANZÖSISCH, UM 1900 (FRÜHFORM DER FARBIGEN KNÖPFE WIE ABB. S. 55 OBEN)

SMALL DARK AMETHYSTS, OVAL CABOCHONS, SLENDER BOX BEZEL SETTING, GOLD, MARKS INCOMPLETE. PROBABLY FRENCH, C. 1900 (EARLY FORM OF THE COLORED CUFFLINKS, LIKE FIG. P. 55 TOP)

SEHR KLEINE OVALE KNÖPFE, JEWEILS IN DER MITTE BESETZT MIT EINEM SAPHIR BZW. BRILLANTEN, GOLD, GENARBT, DEUTSCH, UM 1890–1900, ORIGINALETUI: EDUARD FOEHR, HOFJUWELIER, STUTTGART

VERY SMALL OVAL CUFFLINKS, EACH SET IN THE MIDDLE WITH A SAPPHIRE AND A BRILLIANT-CUT DIAMOND RESPECTIVELY, PEBBLED GOLD. GERMAN, C. 1890–1900, ORIGINAL CASE: EDUARD FOEHR, COURT JEWELER, STUTTGART

ZWEI RUNDE KNÖPFE, KAISERLICH RUSSISCHER DOPPELADLER IM GERIEFTEN GOLDRAND, KETTCHEN-VERBINDUNG, ZWEI PASSENDE KNEBEL, GOLD, SILBER, DIAMANTROSEN, FABERGÉ, MEISTER A. TILLANDER, ST. PETERSBURG, 1880–1909

TWO ROUND CUFFLINKS, DOUBLE-HEADED RUSSIAN IMPERIAL EAGLE IN A RIDGED GOLD RIM, CHAIN CONNECTION, TWO MATCHING TOGGLES, GOLD, SILVER, ROSE-CUT DIAMONDS. FABERGÉ, MASTER JEWELER A. TILLANDER, ST. PETERSBURG, 1880–1909

OVALE KNÖPFE, JEWEILS BESETZT MIT EINEM SAPHIR UND EINEM BRILLANTEN BZW. EINEM RUBIN UND EINEM BRILLANTEN, GOLD, GEHÄMMERT, ENGLISCH ODER FÜR DEN ENGLISCHEN MARKT, UM 1900–1910, ORIGINALETUI: CLARK, 26 OLD BOND STR.

OVAL CUFFLINKS, EACH SET WITH A SAPPHIRE AND BRILLIANT-CUT DIAMOND AND WITH A RUBY AND BRILLIANT-CUT DIAMOND RESPECTIVELY, HAMMERED GOLD, ENGLISH OR FOR THE ENGLISH MARKET, C. 1900–1910, ORIGINAL CASE: CLARK, 26 OLD BOND STREET

ZWEI VERSCHLUNGENE RINGE, JEWEILS BESETZT MIT ZWEI SAPHIREN, EINFACHE KNEBEL, GOLD, GEHÄMMERT, ORIGINALETUI: MORITZ ELIMEYER, HOFJUWELIER, DRESDEN, UM 1890–1900

TWO INTERTWINED RINGS, EACH SET WITH TWO SAPPHIRES, PLAIN TOGGLES, HAMMERED GOLD, ORIGINAL CASE. MORITZ ELIMEYER, COURT JEWELER, DRESDEN, C. 1890–1900

OVALE KNÖPFE MIT »W« UND KAISERKRONE (WILHELM II. VON PREUSSEN), GOLD, SMARAGDE, DIAMANTEN, EMAIL, DEUTSCH, UM 1910

OVAL CUFFLINKS WITH "W" AND IMPERIAL CROWN (WILHELM II OF PRUSSIA), GOLD, EMERALDS, DIAMONDS, ENAMEL. GERMAN, C. 1910

ANTIKE RÖMISCHE DENARE, GOLD, SILBER, MANUFAKTUR ROCCHEGGIANI, ROM, UM 1900

ANTIQUE ROMAN DENARII, GOLD, SILVER. ROCCHEGGIANI MANUFACTURE, ROME, C. 1900

DREIPASSFÖRMIGE KNÖPFE MIT KETTCHEN-VERBINDUNG, DIE BEIDEN GEGENSTÜCKE ZU DEN KNÖPFEN IM FISCHFORM, SILBER, AMETHYSTE, KARL ROTHMÜLLER, UM 1912

TREFOIL-SHAPED CUFFLINKS WITH CHAIN CONNECTION, BOTH BACKS FISH-SHAPED, SILVER, AMETHYSTS. KARL ROTHMÜLLER, C. 1912

DAVIDSTERN, MONOGRAMM UND HEBRÄISCHE SCHRIFTZEICHEN, GOLD, EMAIL, LONDON, 1905

STAR OF DAVID, MONOGRAM AND HEBRAIC CHARACTERS, GOLD, ENAMEL. LONDON, 1905

»W« MIT KAISERKRONE (WILHELM II. VON PREUSSEN), GOLD,
EMAIL, DIAMANTEN, DEUTSCH, UM 1912

"W" WITH IMPERIAL CROWN (WILHELM II OF PRUSSIA), GOLD,
ENAMEL, DIAMONDS. GERMAN, C. 1912

ENGELCHEN MIT PFEIL UND BOGEN, METALL VERGOLDET,
ORIGINALETUI, MONOGRAMMIERT »G.V.R« MIT KRONE,
GARRARD, HOFJUWELIER DES ENGLISCHEN KÖNIGS, UM 1910

CHERUB WITH BOW AND ARROW, GILDED METAL, ORIGINAL CASE,
MONOGRAMMED "G.V.R" WITH CROWN. GARRARD, ROYAL
BRITISH COURT JEWELER, C. 1910

OVALE KNÖPFE MIT WAPPEN, BUCHSTABEN »AE«, KRONE UND DEVISE »ICH DIEN«, GOLD, DIAMANTROSEN, UM 1890–1900

OVAL CUFFLINKS WITH COAT OF ARMS, LETTERS "AE," CROWN AND DEVICE "ICH DIEN" (I SERVE), GOLD, ROSE-CUT DIAMONDS, C. 1890–1900

JUGENDSTILKNÖPFE, FESTE GEWÖLBTE STEGE, GOLD, USA, UM 1900

ART NOUVEAU CUFFLINKS, CONVEX RIGID BARS, GOLD, USA, C. 1900

SCHALENFÖRMIGE KNÖPFE MIT PFERDEPORTRÄTS, FESTE STEGE, GOLD, USA, UM 1900

CONCAVE CUFFLINKS WITH HORSE PORTRAITS, RIGID BARS, GOLD. USA, C. 1900

VIER SPITZOVALE KNÖPFE MIT KETTCHEN-VERBINDUNG, GOLD, EMAIL, FRIEDLÄNDER, BERLIN, UM 1910

FOUR POINTED OVAL CUFFLINKS WITH CHAIN CONNECTION, GOLD, ENAMEL. FRIEDLÄNDER, BERLIN, C. 1910

KLEINE, DUNKELGRÜNE TURMALINE, OVALE
CABOCHONS, SCHMALE GOLDFASSUNG,
KETTCHEN-VERBINDUNG, DEUTSCH ODER
ÖSTERREICHISCH, UM 1900–1910 (FRÜHFORM
DER FARBIGEN KNÖPFE, DIE NUR VOM STEIN-
MATERIAL BESTIMMT SIND)

SMALL DARK GREEN TOURMALINES, OVAL
CABOCHONS, SLENDER GOLD SETTING, CHAIN
CONNECTION. GERMAN OR AUSTRIAN,
C. 1900–1910 (EARLY FORM OF THE COLORED
CUFFLINKS WHICH ARE DEFINED SOLELY BY
THE STONE MATERIAL)

ZU ABB. S. 39 OBEN GEHÖRIGES
ORIGINALES KAISERLICHES
GESCHENKETUI, ROTES LEDER
MIT IN GOLD GEPRÄGTEM
KAISERLICHEM DOPPELADLER

RELATED TO FIG. P. 39 TOP:
ORIGINAL IMPERIAL GIFT
CASE, RED LEATHER WITH
GOLD EMBOSSED DOUBLE-
HEADED IMPERIAL EAGLE

QUADRATISCHE KNÖPFE MIT EINFACHEN KNEBELN,
ROTES EMAIL ÜBER GUILLOCHIERTEM GRUND, IN DEN
ECKEN JE EINE DIAMANTROSE, GOLD, FABERGÉ, MEISTER
ERIK AUGUST KOLLIN, ST. PETERSBURG, 1899–1908

SQUARE CUFFLINKS WITH PLAIN TOGGLES, RED ENAMEL
OVER GUILLOCHÉ GROUND, IN THE CORNERS ONE
DIAMOND-CUT ROSE EACH, GOLD. FABERGÉ, MASTER
JEWELER ERIK AUGUST KOLLIN, ST. PETERSBURG, 1899–1908

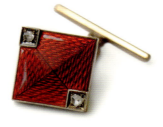 

KOSTBARE MANSCHETTENKNÖPFE
VOM ENDE DES 19. JAHRHUNDERTS BIS HEUTE

PRECIOUS CUFFLINKS FROM THE END
OF THE 19TH CENTURY TO THE PRESENT DAY

1880–1919

1920–1939

1940–1959

1960–1979

1980–2015

SMOKINGGARNITUR, BESTEHEND AUS EINEM PAAR
MANSCHETTEN- UND ZWEI HEMDKNÖPFEN, GOLD, ROSA
KORALLEN, WOHL ENGLAND, UM 1920?

DRESS-COAT JEWELRY SET CONSISTING OF A PAIR OF CUFFLINKS
AND TWO SHIRT STUDS, GOLD, PINK CORAL. PROBABLY ENGLAND,
C. 1920?

»GENTLEMEN'S PLEASURE«, GOLD, EMAIL, ENGLAND,
HENRY GRIFFITH & SONS, 1927

"GENTLEMEN'S PLEASURE," GOLD, ENAMEL. ENGLAND,
HENRY GRIFFITH & SONS, 1927

FLUGWILD (REBHUHN, SCHNEPFE, ENTE, ERPEL), GOLD, GRAVIERTER UND BEMALTER BERGKRISTALL, DEUTSCH, UM 1920

GAME BIRDS (PARTRIDGE, SNIPE, DUCK, DRAKE), GOLD, ENGRAVED AND PAINTED ROCK CRYSTAL. GERMAN, C. 1920

VIER ACHTECKIGE KNÖPFE MIT GEOMETRISCHEN FELDERN, PLATIN, DIAMANTEN, ONYX, FRANKREICH, UM 1930

FOUR OCTAGONAL CUFFLINKS WITH GEOMETRIC FIELDS, PLATINUM, DIAMONDS, ONYX. FRANCE, C. 1930

VIER RUNDE KNÖPFE, JEWEILS MIT ZWEI INEINANDER VERSCHRÄNKTEN WINKELN, PLATIN, SAPHIRE, DIAMANTEN, FRANKREICH, UM 1930

FOUR ROUND CUFFLINKS, EACH WITH TWO INTERTWINED RIGHT ANGLES, PLATINUM, SAPPHIRES, DIAMONDS. FRANCE, C. 1930

FRACKGARNITUR, BESTEHEND AUS EINEM PAAR MANSCHETTEN-, DREI HEMD- UND VIER WESTENKNÖPFEN, GOLD, PLATIN, E. A. DREHER & SON, NEWARK, N. J., ETUI VON KREMENTZ, USA, UM 1920–1930

DRESS-COAT JEWELRY SET CONSISTING OF A PAIR OF CUFFLINKS, THREE SHIRT STUDS AND FOUR VEST BUTTONS, GOLD, PLATINUM. E. A. DREHER & SON, NEWARK, N. J., CASE FROM KREMENTZ, USA, C. 1920–1930

FRACKGARNITUR, BESTEHEND AUS EINEM PAAR MANSCHETTEN- UND ZWEI HEMDKNÖPFEN, PLATIN, MONDSTEINE, GRAUE PERLEN, CARTIER, PARIS, UM 1930

DRESS-COAT JEWELRY SET CONSISTING OF A PAIR OF CUFFLINKS AND TWO SHIRT STUDS, PLATINUM, MOONSTONES, GRAY PEARLS. CARTIER, PARIS, C. 1930

VIER KNÖPFE MIT SAPHIREN, DIAMANTEN,
BERGKRISTALLEN, BEFWES, STOCKHOLM, UM 1930

FOUR CUFFLINKS WITH SAPPHIRES, DIAMONDS,
ROCK CRYSTALS. BEFWES, STOCKHOLM, C. 1930

RAUTENFÖRMIGE JUGENDSTILKNÖPFE, MONDSTEINE, GOLD,
KARL ROTHMÜLLER, UM 1920

DIAMOND-SHAPED ART NOUVEAU CUFFLINKS, MOONSTONES,
GOLD. KARL ROTHMÜLLER, C. 1920

MEERESSCHNECKEN, STERLINGSILBER, GEORG JENSEN,
ENTWURF: HENRY DILSTRUP, DÄNEMARK, UM 1932

CONCHES, STERLING SILVER, GEORG JENSEN, DESIGN:
HENRY DILSTRUP, DENMARK, C. 1932

FRACK- BZW. TRAUERKNÖPFE, WEISSGOLD, ONYX, DIAMANTEN, FRANKREICH, UM 1930

DRESS-COAT OR MOURNING CUFFLINKS, WHITE GOLD, ONYX, DIAMONDS. FRANCE, C. 1930

ZWEI RUNDE SILBER-
TAUSCHIERTE KNÖPFE,
FAHRNER, UM 1920

TWO ROUND SILVER
DAMASCENED CUFFLINKS.
FAHRNER, C. 1920

FRACKGARNITUR, BESTEHEND AUS EINEM PAAR MANSCHETTEN-
UND ZWEI HEMDKNÖPFEN, PLATIN, GOLD, ONYX, DIAMANTEN,
SIGNIERT »JANESICH«, PARIS, UM 1930

DRESS-COAT JEWELRY SET CONSISTING OF A PAIR OF CUFFLINKS
AND TWO SHIRT STUDS, PLATINUM, GOLD, ONYX, DIAMONDS,
SIGNED "JANESICH." PARIS, C. 1930

HERRENSCHMUCKSET, BESTEHEND AUS VIER WESTEN-, EINEM PAAR MANSCHETTEN- UND ZWEI HEMDKNÖPFEN, WEISSGOLD, ONYX, DIAMANTEN, ORIGINALETUI: GARRARD, KÖNIGLICHER HOFJUWELIER, LONDON, UM 1920

MEN'S JEWELRY SET CONSISTING OF FOUR VEST BUTTONS, A PAIR OF CUFFLINKS, AND TWO SHIRT STUDS, WHITE GOLD, ONYX, DIAMONDS. ORIGINAL CASE: GARRARD, ROYAL COURT JEWELER, LONDON, C. 1920

SMOKINGGARNITUR, BESTEHEND AUS EINEM PAAR MAN-
SCHETTEN- UND VIER HEMDKNÖPFEN, PLATIN, SAPHIRE,
DIAMANTEN, PARIS, CARTIER, UM 1930

TUXEDO JEWELRY SET CONSISTING OF A PAIR OF CUFFLINKS
AND FOUR SHIRT STUDS, PLATINUM, SAPPHIRES, DIAMONDS.
PARIS, CARTIER, C. 1930

CEYLON-SAPHIRE, GROSSE OVALE CABOCHONS,
SCHMALE GOLDFASSUNG, WIEN, VOR 1922

CEYLON SAPPHIRES, LARGE OVAL CABOCHONS,
SLENDER GOLD SETTING. VIENNA, BEFORE 1922

KNÖPFE MIT JEWEILS ZWEI KREISRUNDEN SCHEIBEN
MIT HELLBLAUEM, DURCHSCHEINENDEM EMAIL AUF
GUILLOCHIERTEM FOND UND WEISS EMAILLIERTEM
RAND, DIAMANTEN, GOLD, UM 1910–1920

CUFFLINKS, EACH FEATURING TWO CIRCULAR DISCS
EACH WITH LIGHT BLUE, TRANSLUCENT ENAMEL ON
A GUILLOCHÉ GROUND AND A WHITE ENAMELED RIM,
DIAMONDS, GOLD, C. 1910–1920

RUNDE KNÖPFE MIT ZWEI VERSCHIEDENEN RÖMISCHEN MOSAIKEN (TYPISCHE REISEANDENKEN), SILBER, ONYX, ITALIEN, UM 1920

ROUND CUFFLINKS WITH TWO DIFFERENT ROMAN MOSAICS (TYPICAL TRAVEL SOUVENIRS), SILVER, ONYX, ITALY, C. 1920

VIER ART-DÉCO-KNÖPFE MIT FARBIGEN EMAILEINLAGEN, GOLD, KARL ROTHMÜLLER, UM 1920

FOUR ART DECO CUFFLINKS WITH COLORED ENAMEL INLAYS, GOLD. KARL ROTHMÜLLER, C. 1920

FRACKGARNITUR, BESTEHEND AUS EINEM PAAR MANSCHETTEN- UND VIER HEMDKNÖPFEN, GOLD, EMAIL, BAYERISCHE PERLEN, THEODOR HEIDEN, MÜNCHEN, UM 1920

DRESS-COAT JEWELRY SET CONSISTING OF A PAIR OF CUFFLINKS AND FOUR SHIRT STUDS, GOLD, ENAMEL, BAVARIAN PEARLS. THEODOR HEIDEN, MUNICH, C. 1920

RUNDE, VIERFARBIGE KNÖPFE, GOLD, OLIVIN, CITRIN, CITRIN, AQUAMARIN, THEODOR HEIDEN, MÜNCHEN, UM 1930

ROUND, FOUR-COLOR CUFFLINKS, GOLD, OLIVINE, CITRINE, CITRINE, AQUAMARINE. THEODOR HEIDEN, MUNICH, C. 1930

EULEN, SILBER VERGOLDET,
GRANATE, USA, UM 1920

OWLS, GILDED SILVER,
GARNETS, USA, C.1920

JAGDBARES WILD (GEMSE, REHBOCK, FASAN, AUERHAHN), GOLD,
HOLZ, ELFENBEIN, ORIGINALETUI: EMIL JÄGER, PRAG, UM 1930

GAME (CHAMOIS, ROEBUCK, PHEASANT, WOOD GROUSE), GOLD,
WOOD, IVORY. ORIGINAL CASE: EMIL JÄGER, PRAGUE, C.1930

HEMDKNÖPFE, GOLD, PERLEN, ONYX, DEUTSCH (PASSENDE MANSCHETTEN- UND WESTENKNÖPFE VERSCHOLLEN), JUWELIER RUMBORG, BARMEN, UM 1920

SHIRT STUDS, GOLD, PEARLS, ONYX. GERMAN, (WHEREABOUTS OF MATCHING CUFFLINKS UNKNOWN), RUMBORG JEWELRY, BARMEN, C. 1920

CHAUFFEUR MIT MÜTZE, BRILLE UND HUPE, GOLD, SAPHIRE, UM 1920

CHAUFFEUR WITH CAP, GLASSES AND HORN, GOLD, SAPPHIRES, C. 1920

KNÖPFE MIT ÄGYPTISCHEN MOTIVEN, OVALE, FLACH GEWÖLBTE SCHEIBE MIT ANKH-ZEICHEN AUS BLAUEM, ROTEM UND WEISSEM GRUBEN-SCHMELZEMAIL, KNEBEL IN FORM EINES MUMIEN-SARKOPHAGS, BLAU, WEISS UND ROT EMAILLIERT, GOLD, EMAIL, GEST. »18K« (WOHL USA) UND »HIBOU« (FRANZÖSISCHE NACH-PUNZIERUNG), WOHL 1920ER-JAHRE

CUFFLINKS WITH EGYPTIAN MOTIFS, OVAL, SLIGHTLY CURVED DISC WITH ANKH SYMBOL OUT OF BLUE, RED, AND WHITE CHAMP-LEVÉ, TOGGLE IN THE SHAPE OF AN EGYPTIAN SARCOPHAGUS, WHITE AND RED ENAMELED, GOLD, ENAMEL, STAMPED "18K" (PROBABLY USA) AND "HIBOU" (SUBSEQUENT FRENCH HALLMARK). PROBABLY 1920S

GESCHENKKNÖPFE VON KÖNIG GUSTAV V. VON SCHWEDEN, HELLBLAU EMAILLIERTES MONO-GRAMM MIT GOLDENER KRONE IN OVALEM, WEISS EMAILLIERTEM RAHMEN, GOLD, EMAIL UND RUBINE, MEISTERZEICHEN »C.G.H«, STAATSPUNZE, »18K«, »N8« (JAHRESPUNZE FÜR 1939)

COMMEMORATIVE CUFFLINKS FROM KING GUSTAV V OF SWEDEN, LIGHT BLUE ENAMELED MONOGRAM WITH GOLDEN CROWN IN AN OVAL, WHITE ENAMELED FRAME, GOLD, ENAMEL, AND RUBIES, MAKER'S MARK "C.G.H," OFFICIAL HALLMARK "18K", "N8" (HALLMARK FOR THE YEAR 1939)

KOSTBARE MANSCHETTENKNÖPFE
VOM ENDE DES 19. JAHRHUNDERTS BIS HEUTE

PRECIOUS CUFFLINKS FROM THE END
OF THE 19TH CENTURY TO THE PRESENT DAY

1880–1919

1920–1939

1940–1959

1960–1979

1980–2015

MANSCHETTENKNÖPFE UND KRAWATTENNADEL MIT
STERNZEICHEN KREBS, KERAMIK, VERGOLDETES METALL,
WEDGWOOD STRATTON, ENGLAND, 1949

CUFFLINKS AND TIE PINS WITH ZODIAC SIGN CANCER, CERAMIC,
GILDED METAL. WEDGWOOD STRATTON, ENGLAND, 1949

GOLDKNOTEN, CARL THOMAS, MÜNCHEN, UM 1970
GOLD KNOTS, CARL THOMAS, MUNICH, C. 1970

EIN PAAR EULEN, GOLD, DIAMANTEN, USA, UM 1950–1960

PAIR OF OWLS, GOLD, DIAMONDS, US, C. 1950–1960

KNÖPFE MIT RENAISSANCEMOTIV, GOLD, GEFASST AUF GOLDRAHMEN, ENGLAND?, UM 1950

CUFFLINKS WITH RENAISSANCE MOTIF, GOLD, SET IN GOLD FRAME, ENGLAND?, C. 1950

ROT-WEISSE BANDACHATE, OVALE CABOCHONS, SILBERFASSUNG,
SPÄTER VERGOLDET, IDAR-OBERSTEIN, UM 1940–1950

RED AND WHITE BANDED AGATES, OVAL CABOCHONS, SILVER
SETTING, SUBSEQUENTLY GILDED. IDAR-OBERSTEIN, C. 1940–1950

RHODONITE, RUNDE CABOCHONS, GOLDFASSUNG,
IDAR-OBERSTEIN, UM 1940

RHODONITES, ROUND CABOCHONS, GOLD SETTING.
IDAR-OBERSTEIN, C. 1940

KNÖPFE MIT JAPANISCHER
LANDSCHAFT AUF KUPFER,
FASSUNG SILBER VERGOLDET,
KOMAI, JAPAN, UM 1950

CUFFLINKS FEATURING
JAPANESE LANDSCAPE ON
COPPER, SETTING GILDED
SILVER. KOMAI, JAPAN, C. 1950

RUNDE KNÖPFE MIT FLORALEM MOTIV, GOLD, EMAIL,
DIAMANTEN, INDIEN, UM 1950

ROUND CUFFLINKS WITH A FLORAL MOTIF, GOLD, ENAMEL,
DIAMONDS. INDIA, C. 1950

S.T. DUPONT, METALL VERGOLDET, STEIN- UND PERLENIMITATE,
FRANKREICH, UM 1950

S.T. DUPONT, GILDED METAL, IMITATION STONES AND PEARLS.
FRANCE, C. 1950

KNÖPFE, DOUBLÉ, KORALLEN (IMITATION?), UM 1950

CUFFLINKS, PLATED, CORALS (IMITATION?), C. 1950

RUNDE KNÖPFE, GOLD, SAPHIRE, PERLMUTT,
WOHL ENGLAND, UM 1950

ROUND CUFFLINKS, GOLD, SAPPHIRES, MOTHER-OF-PEARL.
PROBABLY ENGLAND, C. 1950

KOSTBARE MANSCHETTENKNÖPFE
VOM ENDE DES 19. JAHRHUNDERTS BIS HEUTE

PRECIOUS CUFFLINKS FROM THE END
OF THE 19TH CENTURY TO THE PRESENT DAY

1880–1919

1920–1939

1940–1959

1960–1979

1980–2015

MANSCHETTENKNÖPFE MIT AUSWECHSELBAREN STÄBCHEN,,
GOLD, LAPISLAZULI, ONYX, BOUCHERON, PARIS, UM 1960

CUFFLINKS WITH INTERCHANGEABLE RODS, GOLD,
LAPIS LAZULI, ONYX. BOUCHERON, PARIS, C. 1960

SCHACHBRETT, GOLD, PERLMUTT, LAPISLAZULI,
ENGLAND, UM 1960?

CHESS BOARD, GOLD, MOTHER-OF-PEARL, LAPIS LAZULI.
ENGLAND, C. 1960?

VIER OVALE CABOCHONS, GOLD, SAPHIRE, GEBRÜDER HEMMERLE, E. SPRANGER, SCHWÄBISCH GMÜND, 1970

FOUR OVAL CABOCHONS, GOLD, SAPPHIRES. GEBRÜDER HEMMERLE, E. SPRANGER, SCHWÄBISCH GMÜND, 1970

OVALE CABOCHONS, GOLD, LABRADORITE, DEUTSCH, UM 1960?

OVAL CABOCHONS, GOLD, LABRADORITE. GERMAN, C. 1960?

VIERFARBIGE KNÖPFE, OVALE HOHE CABOCHONS, AMETHYST, SOGENANNTER MADEIRA-TOPAS, TURMALIN, CITRIN, BREITE FASSUNG, GOLD, E. SPRANGER, SCHWÄBISCH GMÜND, UM 1960–1970

FOUR-COLOR CUFFLINKS, HIGH OVAL CABOCHONS, AMETHYST, SO-CALLED MADEIRA TOPAZ, TOURMALINE, CITRINE, WIDE SETTING, GOLD. E. SPRANGER, SCHWÄBISCH GMÜND, C. 1960–1970

FRACKGARNITUR, BESTEHEND AUS EINEM PAAR
MANSCHETTEN- UND DREI HEMDKNÖPFEN, PLATIN,
RUBINE, USA, UM 1960

DRESS-COAT JEWELRY SET CONSISTING OF A PAIR OF
CUFFLINKS AND THREE SHIRT STUDS, PLATINUM, RUBIES.
USA, C.1960

SOGENANNTE CHIRURGENKNÖPFE, DOUBLÉ,
MILANAISE-GEFLECHT, UM 1960

SO-CALLED SURGEON CUFFLINKS, PLATED,
MILANESE MESH, C. 1960

QUADRATISCHE KNÖPFE, GOLD, WAPPEN EINER STUDENTEN-
VERBINDUNG, UM 1970–1990

SQUARE CUFFLINKS, GOLD, COAT OF ARMS OF A STUDENT
ASSOCIATION, C. 1970–1990

SILBER, ONYX, VICTOR MAYER, NACH CARTIER, UM 1960

SILVER, ONYX. VICTOR MAYER, AFTER CARTIER, C. 1960

SOGENANNTE CHIRURGENKNÖPFE, GOLD, SAPHIRE,
SCHWEIZ, UM 1960

SO-CALLED SURGEON CUFFLINKS, GOLD, SAPPHIRES.
SWITZERLAND, C. 1960

 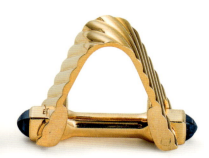

GOLD, RAUCHQUARTZE, UMKLAPPMECHANIKEN MIT
AUFGESETZTEM STEINBOCK, DEUTSCH, UM 1960

GOLD, SMOKY QUARTZES, FOLD-DOWN MECHANISM
SURMOUNTED BY IBEX. GERMAN, C. 1960

GOLDENE JAGDTROPHÄEN
MIT HIRSCHGRANDELN,
UM 1960

GOLDEN HUNTING TROPHIES
WITH DEER CANINES, C. 1960

BLAUE ÄGYPTISCHE SKARABÄEN, GLASIERTE KERAMIK,
SILBER VERGOLDET, UM 1960

BLUE EGYPTIAN SCARABS, GLAZED CERAMIC,
GILDED SILVER, C. 1960

FRACKGARNITUR, BESTEHEND AUS EINEM PAAR MANSCHETTEN-
UND DREI HEMDKNÖPFEN, WEISSGOLD, DIAMANTEN, GEBRÜDER
HEMMERLE, E. SPRANGER, SCHWÄBISCH GMÜND, UM 1960

DRESS-COAT JEWELRY SET CONSISTING OF A PAIR OF CUFFLINKS
AND THREE SHIRT STUDS, WHITE GOLD, DIAMONDS. GEBRÜDER
HEMMERLE, E. SPRANGER, SCHWÄBISCH GMÜND, C. 1960

ZWEI PHÖNIXE, JAPAN,
SAMURAI-APPLIQUEN,
GOLD, MONTIERUNG
MAX POLLINGER, UM 1970

TWO PHOENIXES. JAPAN,
SAMURAI APPLIQUÉS, GOLD,
MOUNT BY MAX POLLINGER,
C. 1970

ZWEI INDISCHE TIGER-
KRALLEN, GOLD, UM 1960

TWO INDIAN TIGER CLAWS,
GOLD, C. 1960

GOLDENER DRACHE MIT
FLÜGEL AUF ROTEM
EMAILGRUND, SPANIEN,
SIGNIERT »MASIERA«,
UM 1960

WINGED GOLDEN DRAGON
ON RED ENAMEL GROUND,
SPAIN, SIGNED "MASIERA,"
C. 1960

OVALE CABOCHONS MIT
GEPUNKTETEM RAND,
GOLD, ACHAT, DEUTSCH,
UM 1960

OVAL CABOCHONS WITH
DOTTED EDGE, GOLD,
AGATE, GERMAN, C. 1960

FRACK-SMOKING-GARNITUR, BESTEHEND AUS EINEM PAAR MANSCHETTEN- UND DREI BZW. VIER HEMDKNÖPFEN, GOLD GRANULIERT, DIAMANTEN, PERLMUTT, THEODOR HEIDEN, MÜNCHEN, UM 1960

DRESS-COAT/TUXEDO JEWELRY SET CONSISTING OF A PAIR OF CUFFLINKS AND THREE OR FOUR SHIRT STUDS, GRANULATED GOLD, DIAMONDS, MOTHER-OF-PEARL. THEODOR HEIDEN, MUNICH, C. 1960

VIER RUNDE KNÖPFE MIT STRAHLENFÖRMIG ANGEFÜGTEN, GESTIELTEN GOLDKÜGELCHEN, CITRINE, SOGENANNTE MADEIRA-TOPASE, GOLD, HANNS ROTHMÜLLER, UM 1965

FOUR ROUND CUFFLINKS WITH RADIALLY ATTACHED GOLD BEADS ON STEMS, CITRINE, SO-CALLED MADEIRA TOPAZES, GOLD, HANNS ROTHMÜLLER, C. 1965

RECHTECKIGE, VIERFARBIGE KNÖPFE, GOLD, CITRIN, ROSA TURMALIN, TURMALIN, AMETHYST, THEODOR HEIDEN, MÜNCHEN, UM 1970

RECTANGULAR FOUR-COLOR CUFFLINKS, GOLD, CITRINE, PINK TOURMALINE, TOURMALINE, AMETHYST. THEODOR HEIDEN, MUNICH, C. 1970

FUCHSKÖPFE AUF GRÜNEM GRUND, GOLD, EMAIL, THEODOR HEIDEN, MÜNCHEN, UM 1960

FOX HEADS ON A GREEN GROUND, GOLD, ENAMEL. THEODOR HEIDEN, MUNICH, C. 1960

RUNDE KNÖPFE »SCHWALBEN«, BERGKRISTALL GRAVIERT, BEMALT, TOMBAK VERGOLDET, ORIGINALETUI: ANTON JANICH, MÜNCHEN, UM 1960

ROUND "SWALLOW" CUFFLINKS, ENGRAVED AND PAINTED ROCK CRYSTAL, GILDED TOMBAC, ORIGINAL CASE: ANTON JANICH, MUNICH, C. 1960

MOOSACHATE?, DOUBLÉ,
DEUTSCH, UM 1970

MOSS AGATES?, PLATED.
GERMAN, C. 1970

OVALE CABOCHONS, GOLD,
MONDSTEINE SRI LANKA,
UM 1960–1970

OVAL CABOCHONS, GOLD,
MOONSTONES. SRI LANKA,
C. 1960–1970

AMETHYSTE, DOUBLÉ,
DEUTSCH, UM 1970

AMETHYSTS, PLATED.
GERMAN, C. 1970

½ SCHWEIZER FRANKEN,
SILBER, 1968

SWITZERLAND ½ FRANC,
SILVER, 1968

DUNHILL, METALL PLATTIERT, LAPISLAZULI-IMITAT,
ENGLAND, UM 1970

DUNHILL, PLATED METAL, IMITATION LAPIS LAZULI,
ENGLAND, C. 1970

GRAVIERTE KNÖPFE, GOLD,
LAPISLAZULI, UM 1970

ENGRAVED CUFFLINKS,
GOLD, LAPIS LAZULI, C. 1970

KNÖPFE AUS ORIGINAL
ROLEX-ARMBAND, GOLD,
DIAMANTEN, UM 1960

CUFFLINKS MADE OF
ORIGINAL ROLEX
BRACELET, GOLD,
DIAMONDS, C. 1960

DREI KRONEN AUF BLAUEM GRUND, DOUBLÉ, SCHWEDEN,
UM 1960

THREE CROWNS ON BLUE GROUND, PLATED. SWEDEN,
C. 1960

Kostbare Manschettenknöpfe
vom Ende des 19. Jahrhunderts bis heute

Precious Cufflinks from the End
of the 19th Century to the Present Day

1880–1919

1920–1939

1940–1959

1960–1979

1980–2015

WEISSGOLDKNOTEN,
ENGLAND, UM 1990

WHITE GOLD KNOTS.
ENGLAND, C. 1990

KLASSISCHE WEISSGOLD-
ABENDKNÖPFE, CABOCHONS,
DIAMANTEN, SAPHIRE,
DEUTSCH, UM 1980

CLASSIC WHITE GOLD
EVENING CUFFLINKS,
CABOCHONS, DIAMONDS,
SAPPHIRES. GERMAN, C. 1980

RUNDE KNÖPFE, WEISSGOLD
MATTIERT, BRILLANTEN, DAZU
PASSENDER ANSTECKKNOPF,
UM 1980

ROUND CUFFLINKS, MATTE
WHITE GOLD, BRILLIANT-CUT
DIAMONDS, WITH MATCHING
PIN, C. 1980

LAPIS-VIERKANT, GOLD,
LAPISLAZULI, UM 1980

LAPIS SQUARE, GOLD,
LAPIS LAZULI, C. 1980

ZARENWAPPEN, GOLD,
EMAIL, DIAMANTEN,
RUSSLAND, UM 1990

RUSSIAN IMPERIAL COAT
OF ARMS, GOLD, ENAMEL,
DIAMONDS. RUSSIA, C. 1990

TREPPENFÖRMIG
ABGESTUFTE KNÖPFE,
CABOCHONS, GOLD,
SAPHIRE, DEUTSCH, UM 1980

STEPPED CUFFLINKS,
CABOCHONS, GOLD,
SAPPHIRES. GERMAN, C. 1980

TONNENFÖRMIGE KNÖPFE, SILBER, EBENHOLZ, UM 1980

BARREL-SHAPED CUFF-LINKS, SILVER, EBONY, C. 1980

VIER OVALE CABOCHONS, GOLD, SMARAGDE, GEBRÜDER
HEMMERLE, J. SPRANGER, SCHWÄBISCH GMÜND, 1980

FOUR OVAL CABOCHONS, GOLD, EMERALDS. GEBRÜDER
HEMMERLE, J. SPRANGER, SCHWÄBISCH GMÜND, 1980

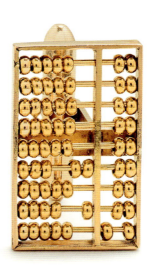

ABAKUS-PAAR, GOLD, UM 1990

PAIR OF ABACUS CUFFLINKS, GOLD, C. 1990

S.T. DUPONT, METALL, GOLD PLATTIERT, UM 1980

S.T. DUPONT, METAL, PLATED GOLD, C. 1980

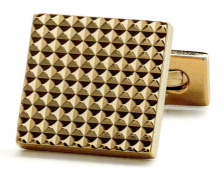

ZWEI RUNDKNÖPFE, KONZENTRISCH GERIPPT, JEWEILS IN DER MITTE BESETZT MIT EINEM KLEINEN RUBIN, SCHLICHTE GEGENKNÖPFE, GOLD, HANSEN, HAMBURG, 1990

TWO ROUND CUFFLINKS, RIBBED CONCENTRICALLY, EACH SET WITH A SMALL RUBY IN THE MIDDLE, PLAIN ROUND BACKS, GOLD. HANSEN, HAMBURG, 1990

GOLD, ROTE TURMALINE AUF GRÜNEM EMAIL, UMRANDET MIT ZARENWAPPEN, RUSSLAND, UM 1990

GOLD, RED TOURMALINES ON GREEN ENAMEL, WITH THE COAT OF ARMS OF THE TSARS. RUSSIA, C. 1990

FUCHSKÖPFE MIT KLAPPBARER LUNTE, GOLD, WEISSGOLD,
DIAMANTEN, RUBINE, ONYX, JUWELIER FRIEDRICH,
FRANKFURT AM MAIN, UM 1980

FOX HEADS WITH FOLDING BRUSH, GOLD, WHITE GOLD,
DIAMONDS, RUBIES, ONYX. JEWELER FRIEDRICH,
FRANKFURT AM MAIN, C. 1980

KNÖPFE IN SCHILDKRÖTENFORM, GOLD, DIAMANTEN,
USA, UM 1980

TURTLE-SHAPED CUFFLINKS, GOLD, DIAMONDS. USA, C. 1980

OVALE KNÖPFE, JEWEILS RÜCKSEITIG GRAVIERT UND BEMALT MIT EINER FLIEGENDEN
WILDENTE, GOLD, BERGKRISTALL, THEODOR HEIDEN, MÜNCHEN, UM 1990

OVAL CUFFLINKS, EACH ENGRAVED ON THE VERSO AND PAINTED WITH A
WILD DUCK IN FLIGHT, GOLD, ROCK CRYSTAL. THEODOR HEIDEN, MUNICH, C. 1990

KNÖPFE MIT WILDSCHWEINEN, SILBER, GEGOSSEN UND ZISELIERT, DEUTSCH,
UM 1980

CUFFLINKS WITH WILD BOARS, SILVER, CAST AND CHASED. GERMAN, C. 1980

RUNDE KNÖPFE MIT JE EINEM MORGENSTERN, GOLD, DEUTSCH,
UM 1990

ROUND CUFFLINKS, EACH WITH A SPIKED MACE, GOLD. GERMAN, C. 1990

MONDSTEIN, KAMEEN, GOLD, WEISSER EMAILRAND,
EINFACHE KNEBEL, HANSEN, HAMBURG, 1992

MOONSTONE, CAMEOS, GOLD, WHITE ENAMEL RIM,
PLAIN TOGGLES. HANSEN, HAMBURG, 1992

FRACKGARNITUR, BESTEHEND AUS EINEM PAAR
MANSCHETTEN- UND DREI HEMDKNÖPFEN, GOLD, ONYX,
DIAMANTEN, THEODOR HEIDEN, MÜNCHEN, UM 1980

DRESS-COAT JEWELRY SET CONSISTING OF A PAIR OF
CUFFLINKS AND THREE SHIRT STUDS, GOLD, ONYX,
DIAMONDS. THEODOR HEIDEN, MUNICH, C. 1980

OVALE KNÖPFE, JEWEILS BESETZT MIT EINER
»KAFFEEBOHNE«, GOLD, ONYX, THEODOR HEIDEN,
MÜNCHEN, UM 1990

OVAL CUFFLINKS, EACH SET WITH A "COFFEE BEAN,"
GOLD, ONYX. THEODOR HEIDEN, MUNICH, C. 1990

OVALE KNÖPFE MIT GRÜNEN
VIERKANTSTÄBEN AUS
NEPHRIT, SOGENANNTER
RUSSISCHER JADE, GOLD,
HANNS ROTHMÜLLER,
UM 1980

OVAL CUFFLINKS WITH
SQUARE GREEN BARS OF
NEPHRITE, SO-CALLED
RUSSIAN JADE, GOLD. HANNS
ROTHMÜLLER, C. 1980

KNÖPFE AUS KORALLE ORANGE, ZUR KUGEL GESCHLIFFEN,
ZWEI SAPHIR-CABOCHONS, GELBGOLDSTEGE, ENTWURF:
ERWIN LANG, WIEN, UM 1920, HOFJUWELIER A. E. KÖCHERT,
WIEN, SALZBURG, 2015

SPHERICALLY CUT CUFFLINKS OF ORANGE CORAL,
TWO SAPPHIRE CABOCHONS, YELLOW GOLD BARS, DESIGN:
ERWIN LANG, VIENNA, C. 1920, COURT JEWELER A. E. KÖCHERT,
VIENNA, SALZBURG, 2015

KARTENSPIEL, GOLD, RUBINE, ONYX, DIAMANTEN,
ITALIEN, O. J.

DECK OF CARDS, GOLD, RUBIES, ONYX, DIAMONDS.
ITALY, N. D.

105

ZWEI KNÖPFE MIT UNRUH
UNTER GLAS, SILBER,
SCHWEIZ, UM 2000

TWO CUFFLINKS WITH
BALANCE WHEEL
UNDER GLASS, SILVER.
SWITZERLAND, C. 2000

S.T. DUPONT, METALL,
WEISSGOLD PLATTIERT,
PARIS, UM 1980

S.T. DUPONT, METAL,
PLATED GOLD, PARIS, C. 1980

MANSCHETTENKNÖPFE FÜR
ENGE MITARBEITER DES
BRITISCHEN RENNFAHRERS
JACK BRABHAM, METALL
VERGOLDET, ENGLAND,
UM 2000

CUFFLINKS FOR CLOSE
COLLEAGUES OF THE BRITISH
RACING DRIVER JACK
BRABHAM, GILDED METAL.
ENGLAND, C. 2000

ZWEI TOTENKÖPFE, WEISSGOLD, RUBINE, TSAVORITE, DIAMANTEN, ITALIEN, UM 2010

TWO SKULLS, WHITE GOLD, RUBIES, TSAVORITES, DIAMONDS. ITALY, C. 2010

ZWEI ELEFANTEN MIT DIAMANTENKÖPFEN, GOLD, ITALIEN, UM 2010

TWO ELEPHANTS WITH DIAMOND HEADS, GOLD. ITALY, C. 2010

VIER OVALE CABOCHONS MIT BREITEM RAND, PLATIN,
AQUAMARINE, FRANZ HEMMERLE, MÜNCHEN, 2014

FOUR OVAL CABOCHONS WITH WIDE RIM, PLATINUM,
AQUAMARINES. FRANZ HEMMERLE, MUNICH, 2014

VIER OVALE CABOCHONS, PLATIN, TURMALINE,
FRANZ HEMMERLE, MÜNCHEN, 2013

FOUR OVAL CABOCHONS, PLATINUM, TOURMALINES.
FRANZ HEMMERLE, MUNICH, 2013

VIER OVALE CABOCHONS MIT BREITEM RAND, PLATIN,
SCHWARZE SAPHIRE, FRANZ HEMMERLE, MÜNCHEN, 2012

FOUR OVAL CABOCHONS WITH WIDE RIM, PLATINUM, BLACK
SAPPHIRES. FRANZ HEMMERLE, MUNICH, 2012

VIER RUNDE MANSCHETTENKNÖPFE, GOLD, ANTIKE
GRIECHISCHE OBOLE (UM 500 V. CHR.), FRANZ HEMMERLE,
MÜNCHEN, 2005

FOUR ROUND CUFFLINKS, GOLD, ANTIQUE GREEN OBOLS
(C. 500 BC). FRANZ HEMMERLE, MUNICH, 2005

KUGELKNÖPFE, ROSÉGOLD, MONDSTEINE, RENÉSIM, MÜNCHEN, 2015

SPHERICAL CUFFLINKS, ROSÉ GOLD, MOONSTONES, RENÉSIM, MUNICH, 2015

KUGELKNÖPFE, WEISSGOLD MIT SCHWARZEN UND WEISSEN DIAMANTEN, RENÉSIM, MÜNCHEN, 2015

SPHERICAL CUFFLINKS, WHITE GOLD WITH BLACK AND WHITE DIAMONDS, RENÉSIM, MUNICH, 2015

GENTS MANSCHETTENKNÖPFE, OVALE CABOCHONS, MATTES ROSÉGOLD, RUBELITE, RENÉSIM, MÜNCHEN, 2015

MEN'S CUFFLINKS, OVAL CABOCHONS, MATT ROSÉ GOLD, RUBELLITE, RENÉSIM, MUNICH, 2015

LAPISLAZULI, RUND, KISSENFÖRMIG, OHNE FASSUNG, IN DER MITTE BESETZT MIT KLEINEN, IN GOLD GEFASSTEN SMARAGDEN, HANSEN, HAMBURG, 2004

LAPIS LAZULI, ROUND, PILLOW-SHAPED, WITHOUT SETTING, SET IN THE CENTER WITH EMERALDS SET IN GOLD. HANSEN, HAMBURG, 2004

JADE, HELLGRÜN, RUND, KISSENFÖRMIG, OHNE FASSUNG, IN DER MITTE BESETZT MIT KLEINEN, IN GOLD GEFASSTEN RUBINEN, HANSEN, HAMBURG, 2003

JADE, LIGHT GREEN, ROUND, PILLOW-SHAPED, WITHOUT SETTING, IN THE MIDDLE SET WITH RUBIES SET IN GOLD. HANSEN, HAMBURG, 2003

ONYXE, RUND, KISSENFÖRMIG, OHNE FASSUNG, IN DER MITTE BESETZT MIT KLEINEN, IN GOLD GEFASSTEN RUBINEN, HANSEN, HAMBURG, 2005

ONYXES, ROUND, PILLOW-SHAPED, WITHOUT SETTING, SET IN THE MIDDLE WITH SMALL RUBIES SET IN GOLD. HANSEN, HAMBURG, 2005

RHODOCHROSITE, RUND, KISSENFÖRMIG, OHNE FASSUNG,
IN DER MITTE BESETZT MIT KLEINEN, IN GOLD GEFASSTEN
SAPHIREN, HANSEN, HAMBURG, 2007

RHODOCHROSITES, ROUND, PILLOW-SHAPED, WITHOUT SETTING,
SET IN THE MIDDLE WITH SMALL SAPPHIRES SET IN GOLD.
HANSEN, HAMBURG, 2007

KARNEOLE, RUND, KISSENFÖRMIG, OHNE FASSUNG, IN DER
MITTE BESETZT MIT KLEINEN, IN GOLD GEFASSTEN SAPHIREN,
DAZUGEHÖRIG: VIER KLEINE HEMDKNÖPFE GLEICHER ART FÜR
SMOKING, HANSEN, HAMBURG, 2005

CARNELIANS, ROUND, PILLOW-SHAPED, WITHOUT SETTING,
SET IN THE MIDDLE WITH SMALL SAPPHIRES SET IN GOLD;
FOUR MATCHING SMALL SIMILAR SHIRT STUDS FOR A TUXEDO.
HANSEN, HAMBURG, 2005

SOGENANNTE COLORADO-TÜRKISE, RUND, KISSENFÖRMIG,
OHNE SICHTBARE FASSUNG, IN DER MITTE BESETZT MIT
KLEINEN, IN GOLD GEFASSTEN SAPHIREN, GOLD, HANSEN,
HAMBURG, 2001

SO-CALLED COLORADO TURQUOISES, ROUND, PILLOW-SHAPED,
WITHOUT VISIBLE SETTING, SET IN THE MIDDLE WITH SMALL
SAPPHIRES SET IN GOLD, GOLD. HANSEN, HAMBURG, 2001

Ausgewählte Literatur
Selected Bibliography

ARNOLD, Ulli. Die Juwelen Augusts des Starken. München/Munich, Berlin: Koehler & Amelang, 2001

ASHELFORD, Jane. The Art of Dress – Clothes through History 1500–1914. London: National Trust, 1996, Aylesbury: National Trust, 2011

BAINBRIDGE, Henry Charles. Peter Carl Fabergé – Goldsmith and Jeweller to the Russian Imperial Court, mit einem Vorwort von/ with a foreword by Sacheverell Sitwell. London: Hamlyn Publishing Group, 1949, spätere Nachdrucke u. a. von/later reprints available such as New York: Crescent Books, 1979

BAKER, Lillian. Hatpins and Hatpin Holders. An Illustrated Value Guide. Paducah, KY: Collector Books, 1983

BERTRAND, Pascale. Cartier – Le style et l'histoire. Paris: Connaissance des arts, 2013

BONHAMS. The Russian Sale. London, November 26, 2014

BRAY, Elizabeth Irvine. Paul Flato – Jeweler to the Stars. Woodbridge, Suffolk: Antique Collectors' Club Ltd, 2010

BREPOHL, Erhard. Theorie und Praxis des Goldschmieds. München/Munich: Hanser Verlag, 1962, 15. Auflage/15th ed. 2003

BURY, Shirley. Jewellery Gallery, Summary Catalogue. London: Victoria and Albert Museum, 1982

BYRDE Penelope. The Male Image. Men's Fashion in Britain 1300–1970. London: B.T. Batsford Ltd, 1980

CAMPBELL, Duncan, Charlotte REY, Sven EHMANN, Robert KLANTEN. The Craft and the Makers. Tradition with Attitude. Berlin: Die Gestalten Verlag, 2014

CAPPELLIERI, Alba. Twentieth-century Jewellery. From Art Nouveau to Contemporary Design in Europe and the United States. Mailand/Milan: Skira, 2010

CHIARELLI, Caterina. Appesi a un filo. Bottoni alla Galleria del costume di Palazzo Pitti, Livorno: Sillabe, 2007

CHRISTIE'S SALE 2646. The Van Cliburn Collection. New York, Rockefeller Plaza, May 17, 2012

COLEMAN, Elizabeth A. Of Men Only – A Review of Men's and Boys' Fashions, 1750–1975. New York: The Brooklyn Museum, 1975

COLEMAN SPARKE, Cynthia. Russian Decorative Arts. Woodbridge, Suffolk: Antique Collectors' Club Ltd, 2014

CUISENIER, Jean. Costume, coutume. Paris: Editions de la Réunion des musées nationaux, 1987

CUMMING, Valerie. The Visual History of Costume Accessories. London: Costume & Fashion Press, 1998

DAMASE, Jacques (Hrsg./ed.). Premier vestiaire pour l'histoire du costume masculin: Apparat, rites et simulacres. Paris: J. Damase, 1983

DE TINGUY, Isabelle. Haute Couture. Fashion in Detail. The Board of Trustees of the Victoria and Albert Museum. Paris: Editions Place des Victoires, 2013

DESAUTELS, Paul E. Edelsteine, Perlen, Jade. Stuttgart: Kosmos Verlags-GmbH, 1973

Deutsche Goldschmiede-Zeitung (DGZ). Leipzig, seit 1898/from 1898 onward

Hessisches Landesmuseum Darmstadt, Sybille EBERT-SCHIFFERER, Martin HARMS (Hrsg./eds.). Faszination Edelstein. Aus den Schatzkammern der Welt. Mythos, Kunst, Wissenschaft. Bern: Benteli, 1992

EHRET, Gloria. Stilkunde Nr. 38: Manschettenknöpfe. München/Munich: Weltkunst, 2010

EPSTEIN, Diana. Buttons. London: Studio Vista, 1968

EPSTEIN, Diana, Millicent SAFRO: Buttons. New York: Harry N. Abrams, 1991, 2001

FALKENBERG, Regine, Adelheid RASCHE, Christine WAIDEN-SCHLAGER. On Men: Masculine Dress Code from the Ancient Greeks to Cowboys. Berlin: Deutsches Historisches Museum [for] ICOM International Committee for Museums and Collections of Costume, 2005

FALLUEL, Fabienne, Liesel COUVREUR SCHIFFER. Antiquités & Objets d'Art N°37: Les Accessoires de Mode. Paris: Éditions Fabbri, 1992

GERE, Charlotte, Judy RUDOE. Jewellery in the Age of Queen Victoria. A Mirror to the World. London: The British Museum Press, 2010

GORDON, Angie. Twentieth Century Costume Jewellery. Woodbridge, Suffolk: Antique Collectors' Club Ltd, 1990

GRAPPE-ALBERS, Heide (Hrsg./ed.). Begehrte Männer – Dresscodes, die die Welt bedeuten. Hannover: Niedersächsisches Landesmuseum, 2008

GRASSER, Walter, Franz HEMMERLE. Kostbare Krawattennadeln. München/Munich, London, New York: Prestel Verlag, 1990

GZ Goldschmiede Zeitung. Das Magazin für Schmuck und Uhren, 112. Jahrgang/vol. 112. Hamburg: Untitled Verlag und Agentur GmbH & Co. KG, 2015

HABSBURG, Geza von, Alexander von SOLODKOFF. Fabergé – Hofjuwelier der Zaren. Fribourg: Office du Livre, 1979

HABSBURG, Geza von. Fabergé – Hofjuwelier der Zaren. München/Munich: Hirmer Verlag, 1994

HABSBURG, Geza von. Fabergé | Cartier – Rivalen am Zarenhof. München/Munich: Hirmer Verlag, 2013

HART, Harold H. (Hrsg./ed.). Jewelry – A Pictorial Archive of Woodcuts and Engravings (Picture Archives). New York: Dover Publications, 1977/1978 und/and 1981

HASE-SCHMUNDT, Ulrike von, Christianne WEBER-STÖBER, Ingeborg BECKER. Theodor Fahrner – Schmuck zwischen Avantgarde und Tradition. Stuttgart: Arnoldsche, 1990, 2005

HASLINGER, Ingrid. Kunde - Kaiser. Die Geschichte der ehemaligen k. und k. Hoflieferanten. Wien: Schroll, 1996

HAUSER-KÖCHERT Irmgard. Köchert – Imperial Jewellers in Vienna. Jewellery Designs 1810–1940. Florenz/Florence: S.P.E.S. Studio Per Edizioni Scelte, 1990

HOFMAN, Jesek, Paula WAHLE. Führer durch die Sammlungen des Waldes-Museums in Prag-Vrsovic. Prag/Prague, 1919

HORNEKOVÁ, Jana. Art déco Boemia 1918–1939. Katalog/catalogue. Mailand/Milan: Electa, 1996

HUGHES, Graham. Erlesener Schmuck – Ein internationales Handbuch von der Entwicklung der Goldschmiedekunst. Mit hervorragenden Beispielen von 1890 bis heute. Für Goldschmiede, Künstler u. alle Freunde schönen Schmuckes. Ravensburg: Otto Maier Verlag, 1965

Indispensables accessoires: XVIe – XXe siècle, Ville de Paris, Musée de la mode et du costume, Dec. 8, 1983 – Apr. 23, 1984. Paris: Palais Galliera, 1983

JESSEN, Jens. Lächerlichkeit tötet – Wie man die richtigen Manschettenknöpfe findet. Eine kleine Stilkunde, in: Weltkunst 2008, Heft/no. 14, S./pp. 11 ff.

JONAS Susan, Marilyn NISSENSON. Cuff Links. New York: Harry N. Abrams, 1999

KELLEY, Lyngerda, Nancy SCHIFFER. Costume Jewelry – The Great Pretenders. Atglen, PA: Schiffer Publishing, 2002

KITCHEN, R. L., H. SCHRAMM. Le costume masculin. Basel: Les Cahiers Ciba 75, 1958

KÖCHERT, Christoph, Wolfgang und/and Florian. H. E. Köchert: 200 Jahre der Juwelier der Kaiser und Könige – Hof- und Kammerjuwelier und Goldschmied seit 1814. Wien/Vienna, 2011

KOEBNER, F. W. (Hrsg./ed.). Der Gentleman – Ein Brevier für den Herrn von Welt. München/Munich: Rogner & Bernhard, 1976

KRÜNITZ, Johann Georg. Oeconomische Encyklopädie oder allgemeines System der Staats-, Stadt-, Haus- und Landwirtschaft, Bd./vols. 1–205, Brünn/Brno 1787

KUHNEN, Hans-Peter (Hrsg./ed.). AUF und ZU. Von Knöpfen, Schnüren, Reissverschlüssen. Stuttgart: Museum für Volkskultur Schloss Waldenbuch, Württembergisches Landesmuseum, 1994

KUZEL, Vladislav. Das Buch vom Schmuck. Prag/Prague: Artia, 1962

KUZMANOVIC, Natasha. Yard – The Life and Magnificent Jewelry of Raymond C. Yard. Mit einem Vorwort von/Foreword by David Rockefeller. New York: Vendome Press, 2008

KYBALOVA, Ludmila, Petr NOVY, Sarka SIRUCKOVA. The Jablonec Button. Landesmuseum Hannover. Originaltitel: Jablonecký Knoflik. Jablonec, Nisa: Muzeum Skla a Bižuterie, 2007

LAMBRECHTS, Guy-David. Antique Cufflinks 1860–1960. Antwerpen/Antwerp: Selbstverlag/private edition, 2011

LANLLIER, Jean, PINI, Marie-Anne. Fünf Jahrhunderte abendländischer Schmuckkunst. München/Munich: Prestel Verlag, 1971

LEHNERT, Gertrud. Mode. Köln/Cologne: DuMont, 1998

LEIBOLD, Paul. Juwelenfasser-Codex. Fulda: Cre Art, 2011

LEONHARDT, Brigitte, Dieter ZÜHLSDORFF (Hrsg./eds.). Theodor Fahrner – Schmuck zwischen Avantgarde und Tradition, Forum für Europäische Kunst & Kultur. Stuttgart: Arnoldsche, 2006

LIAUT, Jean-Noel, Bertrand PIZZIN. Cuff Links. New York: Assouline Publishing, 2002

LOSCHEK, Ingrid. Mode im 20. Jahrhundert – Eine Kulturgeschichte unserer Zeit. München/Munich: Bruckmann, 1988

LOSCHEK, Ingrid. Accessoires – Symbolik und Geschichte. München/Munich: Bruckmann, 1993

LOSCHEK, Ingrid. Fashion of the Century – Chronik der Mode von 1900 bis heute. München/Munich: Battenberg, 2001

LOSCHEK, Ingrid. Reclams Mode- und Kostümlexikon. Stuttgart: Reclam, 1990, 6. aktualisierte und erweiterte Auflage/6th updated and expanded ed. 2011

MASCETTI, Daniela, Amanda TRIOSSI. Earrings – From Antiquity to the Present. London: Thames & Hudson, 1999; deutsche Ausgabe: Der Ohrring von der Frühzeit bis zur Gegenwart. Frankfurt am Main/Berlin: Propyläen, 1991

MORO, Ginger. European Designer Jewelry. Atglen, PA: Schiffer Publishing, 1995

Musei civici di Padova. Il Tresor Trieste. Gioielli della collezione Trieste e della collezione Sartori Piovene di musei civici di Padova, Katalog/catalogue. Padua, 1992

NADELHOFFER, Hans. Cartier – Jewelers Extraordinary. London: Thames & Hudson, 1984, deutsche Ausgabe/German ed.: Cartier – König der Juweliere. Juwelier der Könige. Herrsching am Ammersee: Schuler, 1984, 1987

O'HARA, Georgina. The Encyclopaedia of Fashion. From 1840 to the 1980s. London: Thames & Hudson, 1989

PEACOCK, John. Männermode – Das Bildhandbuch von der Zeit der Französischen Revolution bis zur Gegenwart. Bern: Haupt Verlag, 1996

PELTASON, Ruth. David Webb – The Quintessential American Jeweler. New York: Assouline Publishers, 2013

PIEPER, Wolfgang. Geschichte der Pforzheimer Schmuckindustrie. Gernsbach: Casimir Katz Verlag, 1989

POYNDER, Michael. The Price Guide to Jewellery 3000 B.C. to 1950 A.D. Woodbridge, Suffolk: Antique Collectors' Club Ltd, 1976, Nachdrucke/reprints 1981, 1985, 1988, 1990

Register of members of the Association of Jewelers, Gold- and Silversmiths of the Imperial-Royal Capital City of Vienna 1902

ROETZEL, Bernhard. Gentleman: A Timeless Fashion. Köln/Cologne: Koenemann, 1999

ROETZEL, Bernhard. Der Gentleman: Handbuch der klassischen Herrenmode. Köln/Cologne: Koenemann, Potsdam: Ullmann, 2014

ROMMENS, Aarnoud (Hrsg./ed.). Symposium 2: Seam & Star – Male Elegance, ModeMuseum Provincie Antwerpen. Symposium. Antwerpen/Antwerp: MoMu, 2010

SCARISBRICK, Diana. Portrait Jewels: Opulence and Intimacy from the Medici to the Romanovs, London: Thames & Hudson, 2011

SCHUMANN, Walter. Edle Steine – Faszination seit Jahrtausenden. München/Munich: BLV Buchverlag, 1992, 2009

SNOWMAN, Abraham Kenneth. The Art of Carl Fabergé. London: Faber & Faber, 1962

SNOWMAN, Abraham Kenneth. The Master Jewelers. New York: Harry N. Abrams, 1990

SOBIK, Helge. Picasso an der Riviera. Düsseldorf: Feymedia Verlag, 2010

SOLODKOFF, Alexander von. Russian Gold and Silverwork 17th–19th Century. New York: Rizzoli, 1981

SOLODKOFF, Alexander von. Masterpieces from the House of Fabergé. New York: Harry N. Abrams, 1989

SOLODKOFF, Alexander von, The Jewel Album of Tsar Nicholas II and A Collection of Private Photographs of the Russian Imperial Family. With an essay by Irina A. Bogatskaya, Curator of the Archives at the State Museums of the Moscow Kremlin, London, Ermitage, 1997

Sotheby's auction house catalogue. Romanov Heirlooms. The Lost Inheritance of Grand Duchess Maria Pavlovna, London, 20 November 2008

SYNDRAM, Dirk. Prunkstücke des Grünen Gewölbes zu Dresden. Leipzig: E. A. Seemann, 2006

SYNDRAM, Dirk. Gems of The Green Vault in Dresden. Leipzig: E. A. Seemann, 2012

TAIT, Hugh. 7000 Years of Jewellery. London: Firefly Books, 2008

TENNENBAUM, Suzanne, Janet ZAPATA. The Jeweled Menagerie: The World of Animals in Gems. London: Thames & Hudson, 2001, 2007

THIEL, Erika. Geschichte der Mode von den Anfängen bis zur Gegenwart. Augsburg: Weltbild, 1990

TOLKIEN, Tracy, Henrietta WILKINSON. A Collector's Guide to Costume Jewelry. Key Styles and how to Recognise them, 1. Auflage/1st ed. in Canada, 2. Auflage/2nd ed. in England, Eastbourne, 1962, London: Thames & Hudson, 1997

UNTRACHT, Oppi. Traditional Jewelry of India. New York: Harry A. Abrams, 1997, London: Thames & Hudson, 1997, 2008

VALLE, Michele della. Jewels and Myths. Woodbridge, Suffolk: Antique Collectors' Club, 2014

Verzeichnis der Mitglieder der Genossenschaft der Juweliere, Gold- u. Silberschmiede der k.k. Reichshaupt- und Residenzstadt Wien. Wien/Vienna, 1902

VEVER, Henri. La bijouterie française au XIXe siècle (1800–1900). Paris: H. Floury Libraire-Editeur, 1906, 1908

VOLPINI, Leonardo. I Gemelli da Polso. Mailand/Milan: Federico Motta Editore, 2001

WAIDENSCHLAGER, Christine, Kunstgewerbemuseum – Staatliche Museen zu Berlin (Hrsg./eds.): Mode – Kunst – Werke 1715 bis heute. Petersberg: Imhof Verlag, 2014

WATERFIELD, Hermione, Christopher FORBES. Fabergé – Imperial Eggs and other Fantasies. New York: Scribner, 1978

ZEGNA, Anna. Ermenegildo Zegna. An Enduring Passion for Fabrics, Innovation, Quality and Style. Mailand/Milan: Skira, 2010

Zur Geschichte der Kostüme. Münchener Bilderbogen, Nr. 296. München/Munich: Braun & Schneider, um/c. 1880

BILDNACHWEIS/IMAGE CREDITS:

A. E. Köchert Juweliere, Salzburg: Seite/page 103 (unten/below)

bpk – Bildagentur für Kunst, Kultur und Geschichte: Seite/page 18

Decker, Anna-Maria, München: Seite/page 28, 29, 30 (rechts, oben/right, above) 31, 34, 35, 36, 37, 38 (oben/above), 40, 41, 42, 43, 45, 46 (oben und Mitte/above and middle), 47 (unten/below), 48, 49, 50, 51, 52 (unten/below), 53, 54 (oben, rechts und Mitte/above, right and middle), 55 (oben/above), 57, 58, 59, 60, 62 (oben und unten/above and below), 63, 64, 65 (oben/above), 67 (oben/above), 73 (oben/above), 74, 79, 80, 81, 82 (unten/below), 84, 85 (unten/below), 86, 94, 96, 98, 99, 108, 109, 110

dpa Picture-Alliance GmbH: Seite/page 15

Friedrich Juwelier, Frankfurt am Main: Seite/page 99 (oben/above)

Getty Images: Seite/page 21 (Photo by CBS Photo Archive/Getty Images), 22 (Photo by Hulton Archive/Getty Images), 23 (Photo by Tim Graham/Getty Images), 25 (Pierre-Philippe Marcou/AFP/Getty Images; Ausschnitt/detail)

Hemmerle, Franz, München: Seite/page 30 (links/left), 52 (oben und unten/above and below), 54 (oben, links und unten/above, left and below), 61 (oben und Mitte/above and middle), 62 (Mitte/middle), 66, 75 (Mitte/middle), 85 (oben/above), 87, 88, 100, 102, 107 (unten/below)

Kiemer, Karin, Hamburg: Seite/page 98, 101, 112, 113

Renésim GmbH, München: Seite/page 111

Schvarcz, Daniel: Seite/page 65 (unten/below), 69

Solodkoff, Alexander von, Barkelsby: Seite/page 30 (rechts, unten/right, below), 33, 38 (unten/below), 39, 46 (unten/below), 47 (oben/above), 55 (Mitte und unten/middle and below)

Struckhoff, Marco, München: Seite/page 45 (oben/above), 52 (Mitte/middle), 61 (unten/below), 67 (unten/below), 68, 71, 72, 73 (unten/below), 75 (oben und unten/above and below), 76, 82 (oben und Mitte/above and middle), 82 (oben und Mitte/above and middle), 83, 89, 90, 91, 93, 95, 97, 103 (oben und mitte/above and middle), 105, 106, 107 (oben/above)

Schrammerstrasse 3
Am Marienhof
80333 München

HEIDEN
KGL. BAYER. HOFGOLDSCHMIED

+49 (0) 89 29 19 030
info@heiden.eu
www.heiden.eu

200 JAHRE
DER JUWELIER DER KAISER
A. E. KÖCHERT

A. E. Köchert
Neuer Markt 15 • 1010 Wien
(43-1) 512 58 28

A. E. Köchert
Alter Markt 15 • 5020 Salzburg
(43-662) 84 33 98

www.koechert.com

Feine Juwelen aus vielen Epochen – Anlagediamanten
Fine Jewellery – Precious Diamonds

Pacellistraße 5 | 80333 München
Telefon: +49 (0) 89 222 702 | info@juwelenhahn.de
www.juwelenhahn.de

Salvatorplatz 2 | 80333 München
Telefon: +49 (0) 89 2420 3450 | info@hahn-schmuck.de
www.hahn-schmuck.de

♛ Carl Weishaupt
HOFJUWELIER GEGR. 1692

Familienunternehmen in 10. Generation, Inh. Florian Biehler, Silberschmiedemeister, spezialisiert auf Juwelen und Silbergefäße vom 17. Jahrhundert bis zur Moderne.

Betreibt im Rahmen der **GALERIE P13** Dokumentationen und Ausstellungen zur Schmuckgeschichte.

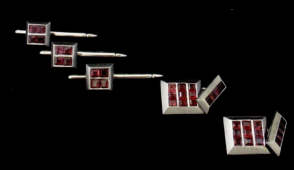

CARL WEISHAUPT | Promenadeplatz 13 | 80333 München | galerie@carlweishaupt.de

Almut Wager

Fine Antique Jewellery

almutwager.de

GALERIE RAUHENSTEIN

ERLESENE ALTE MANSCHETTENKNÖPFE · FINE ANTIQUE CUFFLINKS

Bräuhausstraße 10   80331 München – Munich   Tel. +49 89 22 89 476   r.hovis@t-online.de

MGM

Antiker und erlesener Schmuck

MGM Joker KG · Stiglmaierplatz 2 · 80333 München
Telefon 089/5233660 · mgm@muenzgalerie.de · www.muenzgalerie.de

Ikonen Galerie Dr. Michael Ewenstein

Seit 40 Jahren offerieren wir Liebhabern altrussischer Kunst Ikonen des 16. bis 19. Jahrhunderts sowie Objekte aus Silber und Emaille.

Offering icons dating from the 16th to the 19th century as well as silver and enamel artifacts to connoisseurs of Russian antiques since 40 years.

Ikonen Galerie
Dr. Michael Ewenstein
Knausstrasse. 14
14193 Berlin

Phone +49 30 825 40 51
Mobil +49 172 311 18 81
office@ikonen-ewenstein.de
www.ikonen-ewenstein.de

Manschettenknöpfe, Moskau, ca. 1880–1890
Cufflinks, Moskau, ca. 1880–1890

RENÉSIM
Fine Jewellery

Hundertprozent Individualität.
www.renesim.com

**MANSCHETTENKNÖPFE
AUS DER &-COLLECTION**
Saphir & Jade

M. Hemmerle
Gründer & Creative Director

Individuelles Design & persönliche Beratung | 180 Jahre Familientradition | Höchste Qualität – 100 % Zufriedenheitsgarantie

RENÉSIM steht für Meisterstücke, die so einzigartig sind, wie die Persönlichkeit ihrer Träger. Genau wie die Schmuckstücke der Prêt-à-Porter-Kollektion sind auch individuelle Anfertigungen persönlich, telefonisch oder online erhältlich. Denn Persönlichkeit ist der wahre Luxus.

Wir lassen Ihre Wünsche Realität werden!
renesim GmbH, München | T +49 89 1222 893-0 | service@renesim.com | www.renesim.com

Teilnehmer der Hand Made in Germany Worldtour 2016

ERSCHIENEN IM/PUBLISHED BY
Hirmer Verlag
Nymphenburger Strasse 84
80636 Munich, Germany

AUTOREN/AUTHORS:
Walter Grasser
Franz Hemmerle
Alexander Herzog von Württemberg

REDAKTION/EDITING:
Gabriele Ebbecke, München/Munich

DEUTSCHES LEKTORAT/GERMAN COPY-EDITING:
Anke Beck, München/Munich
Gabriele Ebbecke, München/Munich

DEUTSCHES KORREKTORAT/GERMAN COPY-EDITING:
kultur&kontext, Ilka Backmeister-Collacott, Freiburg, Germany

ENGLISCHE ÜBERSETZUNG/ENGLISH TRANSLATION:
Bram Opstelten, Richmond, Virginia, USA

ENGLISCHES LEKTORAT UND KORREKTORAT/ENGLISH COPY-EDITING AND PROOF-READING:
Jane Michael, München/Munich

HIRMER PROJEKTMANAGEMENT/HIRMER PROJECT MANAGEMENT:
Rainer Arnold
Hannes Halder

GESTALTUNG UND SATZ/LAYOUT AND TYPESETTING:
zwischenschritt, Rainald Schwarz

LITHOGRAFIE/PRE-PRESS AND REPRO:
Reproline Genceller, München/Munich

DRUCK UND BINDUNG/PRINTING AND BINDING:
Printer Trento S.r.l.

PAPIER/PAPER:
Garda Art Matt 170 g/m^2

Printed in Italy

Bibliografische Information der Deutschen Nationalbibliothek
Die Deutsche Nationalbibliothek verzeichnet diese Publikation in der Deutschen Nationalbibliografie;
detaillierte bibliografische Daten sind im Internet über http://dnb.dnb.de abrufbar.
Bibliographic information published by the Deutsche Nationalbibliothek
The Deutsche Nationalbibliothek lists this publication in the Deutsche Nationalbibliografie;
detailed bibliographic data are available on the Internet at http://dnb.dnb.de

Abbildungen Schutzumschlag/Dust jacket images: Siehe Seite 47 und 51/see page 47 and 51
Abbildung Bezug/Cover image: Siehe Seite 89/see page 89
Abbildungen Vorsatz/Endpaper images: Entwurfszeichnungen, Frankreich, um 1920–1930/Design drawings, France, c. 1920–1930
Abbildung Seite 2/3/Image page 2/3: Siehe Seite 75/see page 75
Abbildung Seite 4/5/Image page 4/5: Siehe Seite 69/see page 69
Abbildung Seite 8/Image page 8: Siehe Seite 65/see page 65
Abbildung Seite 10/11/Image page 10/11: Siehe Seite 36/see page 36

© 2016 Hirmer Verlag GmbH, München/Munich; die Autoren/the Authors.

ISBN 978-3-7774-2459-0 (Deutscher Einband/German cover)
ISBN 978-3-7774-2423-1 (Englischer Einband/English cover)

www.hirmerverlag.de
www.hirmerpublishers.com